Activities, Games and Challenges for Learning Outside the Classroom

Volume 2

Activities, Games and Challenges for Learning Outside the Classroom

Volume 2

The Teacher, Playworker, Outdoor Practitioner and Forest School Leader Handbook of Games and Activities

Tracey Maciver

forestschool@hotmail.co.uk

http://forestschoolandoutdoorlearning.com

ISBN 978 1 5272 2802 3

Printed by Short Run Press Ltd, Exeter, Devon

Dedication: To my wonderful children,
Liam, Callum, Marcus, Catty, Sammie and Dan,
Davy my rock, my mother Beryl and
my mother in law Mary for looking after us all

Welcome

Thank you for reading this book, let me introduce myself. Over the years I have worked with a wide range of children of all ages and abilities in the Early Years sector, in primary, secondary and special schools as well as a stint as a Beaver Scout leader. I have been a Forest School Leader for many years and later a Forest School Trainer and an outdoor learning consultant and trainer. I am a parent and a home educator. I have taught children, students and adults and they in turn have taught me back.

Hopefully you will find this book helpful and enjoy many happy times outdoors. Whether you are a teacher, an early year's practitioner, youth leader, play worker, parent, home educator, trainee forest school leader or an old hand you will find something new to try out.

This book is designed to offer practical tips and advice for those using the outdoors as a learning environment. I suggest that you browse my first book 'Activities, Games and Challenges for Learning Outside the Classroom' (2013) ISBN 978 0 95760930 3 which can be obtained from www.forestschoolandoutdoorlearning.co.uk as well as Amazon, eBay and other usual online book outlets. The first book was an introduction to an array of games and activities which can be done outside for both experienced outdoor practitioners as well as those at the start of their journey. The activities sit nicely alongside Forest School sessions as it is always great to have a few planned activities if the children need direction or focus or as standalone activities to incorporate into any outdoor learning session.

After I had finished that book I started to think about all the activities that I wished I had put into it and started writing them down. I have spent the last few years travelling the country doing inset days for schools, nurseries and organisations and that also sprouted a whole new range of ideas which I developed and tried out on many enthusiastic practitioners and children. The best ideas are those that develop from real life situations and some have been developed from observing children and how they utilise what they have in their immediate environment.

I have had such wonderful feedback from many practitioners and teachers using the first book who have found it useful for planning and running activities. One of my favourite calls was from a harried headteacher who asked me to hurry and send more copies of the book as her teachers were rapidly falling out in the staffroom over the one copy they did have.

As the first book was designed to be used by everyone, I did not put in a section on using tools which many people have suggested would be useful, so I am pleased to say that tools, how to use them and how to look after them as well as activities using tools have their own section in this new book. Again, this book, like the first book is set out like a recipe book with one activity per page showing you what preparation is needed, what resources are required to do the activity, who it is suitable for as well as changes which can be made to make it more accessible for others as well as the size of the group it works well with. I also have included at the end of each activity ideas about what we are learning from it to make it easier to link to learning outcomes and planning.

I hope you enjoy this book and find it useful. Please feel free to contact me with any feedback as I love hearing it and I do take on board suggestions.

Introduction

Forest School and Outdoor learning is vital today for children to access a range of skills not commonly taught in schools. The need for children to build their self-esteem and confidence as well as resilience and persistence is one that is sadly often bypassed for result driven data collection. Taking the children outdoors is a relief from pressure often felt by both the children and school staff. Guarding children's mental health as well as that of the adults around them is important for the well-being of our future society. Being outside also has the benefit of promoting the development of personal, social and emotional skills as well as soft skills such as cooperation, working with others, planning and problem solving as well as independence, working on their own initiative and learning how to handle risks and incorporate them into their everyday lives and build resilience making them more open to the idea of trying new things and taking chances in new situations.

Outdoor learning and Forest School has started to be recognised by schools to counter the tremendous stress children are being put under by the current education system. Many schools and settings are now proud to be offering sessions and promote it as beneficial to children's mental health and wellbeing. When I first started on my Forest School journey it was still in its infancy in the UK and many Headteachers questioned my sanity when I told them what I planning to do but a few brave souls got on board and the benefits for both the children and staff were enormous, classes were gelling much better, children who did not shine academically were showing achievements and confidence outside not previously observed by their teachers, children were being cooperative and it was being noticed both back in the school environment as well as in their homelife. Children were also showing increasing care and stewardship for their local environment with a deeper understanding about the impact of actions on nature. They started to engage in their environment and often the trickle effect was felt not only through the school but was also being relayed back and changing family behaviours too. A generation of children being raised to care for the environment may have a profound effect on our future compared to a generation who have not established a positive relationship with the outside world.

Being outside and in touch with nature is a more natural environment for us all. When I step outside into a green environment I immediately feel calmness washing over me and the stresses of the hectic modern lifestyle seeping away. Studies have been done showing that hospital patients make a quicker recovery when they can see nature from their windows rather than a manmade environment. Children become calmer and more observant when outdoors (sometimes after an initial outburst of pent up energy suppressed from always having to use an 'indoor voice'.

According to The Mental Health Foundation, about 1 in 10 children and young people will experience mental health issues including depression, anxiety and conduct disorder with over 70 % of these not having appropriate interventions at a sufficiently early age.

They suggest that the emotional wellbeing of children is just as important as their physical health. Good mental health allows children and young people to develop the resilience to cope with whatever life throws at them and grow into well-rounded, healthy adults and that strategies which will help to keep children and young people well include being in good physical health, eating a balanced diet and getting regular exercise, having time and the freedom to play, indoors and outdoors, going to a school that looks after the wellbeing of all its pupils and taking part in local activities for young people. https://www.mentalhealth.org.uk/a-to-z/c/children-and-young-people

These strategies fit in well with the rise in outdoor education and Forest School provision in this country and abroad.

It is not only children and young people who benefit from being outside and in contact with nature, with 1 in 4 people experiencing significant mental health problems the study has shown that 'green care interventions can provide an increasingly important and cost-effective way of supporting mental health services.'

A study shows that taking part in nature-based activities helps people who are suffering from mental ill-health and can contribute to a reduction in levels of anxiety, stress, and depression and that the use of nature-based interventions can help people suffering from mental ill-health. https://www.gov.uk/government/news/connecting-with-nature-offers-a-new-approach-to-mental-health-care (2016)

Contents

7 – Challenges

1

Running a session outdoors

The perfect Forest School session would be one where you go to the woods with children who are regular visitors having participated in a long-term programme which has taken place over a range of seasons and they are familiar and comfortable within the environment. The children initiate activities themselves and it is entirely a child led session with the adults' role being one of observer and facilitator. ... This is what we strive for and it does happen eventually where children are given the time and space to explore and develop their own self confidence and resilience. Unfortunately many of us live in a world where children are released into the outdoor environment on a short term or infrequent basis and once there if left to their own initiative are flummoxed by what to do with their freedom, run wild, go into Lord of the Flies mode or complain that there is 'nothing to do'

Children (and indeed adults too) will often initially feel nervousness and trepidation at the idea of deciding what they can do and leading their own learning, so it is usually a good idea to start a child's foray to freedom with a range of activities and games which will build their confidence and skills in the outdoor environment. Over time and familiarity, they will become more active in their own learning journey and start to digress into developing their own ideas. One day you will do a session and all your activities will stay in the bag and the children will have been too busy and engaged with their own agendas to be distracted by what you had planned, that is the sign of ultimate success.

Risks and Hazard Awareness

When introducing outdoor learning either in a forest school environment or using woodlands, parklands, beaches, moorlands, school or setting grounds, there are many factors you need to be aware of. Before taking a group outside, make sure that you are comfortable in the outdoor environment yourself. Taking part in training programmes and reading books about the subject can help, but you need to experience it first hand, so get yourself outside. Training can give you knowledge and knowhow but the best way to boost your confidence is to practice ... then practice some more!

Although you can do outdoor learning and forest school activities without undergoing training, I do recommend taking the step to becoming a qualified practitioner. Training courses are available for Forest School through a wide array of trainers. Ask around and get recommendations as to who would be suitable for your needs. My feelings are that nothing beats hands on face to face training, but some companies now offer online training courses which are great if you do not have any accessible trainers near you, but you will still need to practice outside to build your confidence, hone your skills and develop your awareness of the outdoor environment.

If you want your sessions to be successful you will need

to prepare well. Even sessions which you are intending to be mostly free play or wholly child led using only natural found resources still need careful planning. The safety and welfare of the children and accompanying adults and helpers is in your hands so don't leave anything to chance. Try to anticipate any stumbling blocks before you reach them.

The first step you need to take is to visit your area. Risk asses your journey to the outdoor area. What potential hazards could you encounter on the way there? Do you need to cross roads or go through a car park? What measures could you put in place to counter risks? Could you use a rope bus to keep children together or a buddy system? Can you place adults to halt traffic or operate a crossing system? Can you introduce that young people do not go ahead of the lead adult and have a tail adult at the back of the group? For younger children use a long rope and ask the children to hold onto the rope bus. Spread them out so that they do not trip over each other. If you find that the children 'bunch up' too much try to spread them out either by tying knots at regular intervals along the rope for children to hold onto or tying string or ribbons at regular intervals. I like to use rope 'mini buses' with one adult overseeing each 'bus' of about 6-8 children and more children get the opportunity to be the driver and lead but long rope buses are fun too and will become your safety circle at base camp.

If you are working in woodlands rather than on school grounds have a map reference of where you are and entry points for vehicles. Make sure that you have an emergency point of contact who if necessary can direct emergency services to the area you are in. If you are in a remote location, make sure you have contingency plans for getting help if anything goes wrong.

I know this may seem a bit worrying but always prepare for

the worst-case scenario. Always take an emergency bag with you for every session which includes a first aid kit which is fully stocked and in date, a working telephone with emergency contacts, up to date information about the children (and/or adults) in your group concerning allergies and medical needs, any medication which must be administered in an emergency, for example epi pens or inhalers. Please ensure that you are First Aid trained. There are many bespoke first aid courses available for Forest School and outdoors which cover the additional hazards you may encounter in the outdoor environment. Make sure your first aid kit is fully stocked and in date and most importantly to hand if you need it. If it is not your class, make sure that you have talked in depth to the class teacher beforehand. Do you have any children who are likely to run off or be frightened by an earthworm? (Deploy adults accordingly).

When you arrive at your outdoor learning area, risk assess the area and check it making sure that it is debris and litter free. Check that nothing has changed and that no new nasty surprises have appeared since the last time you used the area. As well as looking at ground and eyelevel also look up and check the trees and branches for deadfall and hanging branches. If any trees or areas look particularly hazardous rope off areas not to be entered by the children or young people.

Make sure that your area is suitable for the kind of activities that you have planned or the kind of activities you may think that the children may engage in if they initiate their own play based on your previous knowledge and experience of the group. Check that the immediate and further out areas are litter and debris free and that you are aware of anything that could pose a risk to the children or students in your care. If there are rabbit holes and stinging nettles that children could fall over or hurt themselves on, please make them aware of any potential hazards. If something is particularly hazardous or poses a substantial risk, you may wish to rope off that area or move to a different area completely. Examples of this could be an active wasps nest or hanging branches in trees which could fall. If you cannot deal with the potential hazard, move to a less risky area. However, with lower risks, rather than removing every perceived danger, enable the children to start to learn how to manage risks themselves as part of the learning process. Reinforce boundaries and where children can go during the session. Why not initiate a discussion about boundaries and let the children set their own boundaries? Continually monitor the health and safety of the area you are in and the activities of everybody in the area throughout the session. Remember if you are not happy with the safety of children in the group or even accompanying adults' actions and feel that there is potential for an accident if it continues, do something about it.

Check the weather and windspeed before your session and the forecast for the duration. Do not have sessions under trees or in woodland when there are high winds due to falling branches. Continually monitor the safety in the area throughout the session.

Make sure you have enough help from willing adults to enable the session to take place. (Sometimes an unwilling adult can make the session really challenging work and less enjoyable for all.) Make all adults aware of your expectations for the session and ensure you cover your ratios and maybe add in some more to make a session go smoothly. Allocate different tasks to the adults. Check they are confidence to do so. It would be very challenging for someone with a spider phobia to support children on a bug hunt whereas they might be very happy to supervise the fire area and prepare drinks and a snack for the children on their return to the fire circle. Never push your volunteers into something they are not happy with and never expect someone to do something that you are not prepared to yourself.

Take water to drink and the means to make a hot drink if you are out in chilly weather. If you are outside for a long time take snacks to revive flagging adventurers (but please check for allergies)

Setting boundaries and managing risks

Make sure that you risk assess your trip to the forest school site, your area before the session and ongoing throughout the time you are there in case anything changes. Risk assess every activity in advance, so you are aware of any potential risks and hazards. Ensure your kit is fit for purpose by caring for and checking tools and resources on a regular basis.

During the session make sure that you have sufficient adult helpers to cover the required ratios. Teach children how to manage risks. Make them aware of potential hazards and together think of ways to minimise these risks as part of the learning process. Talk about where children can go during the session and highlight any potentially dangerous areas. Reinforce boundaries throughout the session. When you are confident that the children understand the concept of boundaries you can enable them to set their own boundaries as a group and set their own rules and risk assessments, however it is important that the leader is present to advise and guide during this process. Children will have a better understanding of potential hazards if they have identified them as a group and individually. If children's or adult's behaviour and actions during the session causes worry rather than saying "don't do that!" ask them to explain the potential outcome of their action.

Dressing for the outdoors

It is important to dress suitably for the outdoors. Weather conditions are a principal factor along with the area you will be in. Both Children and adults need to wear long sleeved t-shirts and trousers, warm layers and a waterproof outer layer. Investing in waterproof trousers will make life a lot more comfortable when out in winter and the wet. Fleeces and some manmade fabrics are not resistant to fire sparks so wearing wool and cotton is preferable. Make sure that long hair is tied back, and a hat is worn for warmth or to shade from the sun. The rise of the proliferation of ticks which can cause Lyme disease has necessitated the need to wear long trousers and socks when in a woodland, heath or meadow area. Outdoor conditions can be changeable, even during a short session so I advise using layers which can be added or removed as needed. Check people before a session to ensure that they are suitably dressed and supplement their wardrobe as necessary to ensure their comfort throughout the session. If it is cold do they have enough clothes and layers? Layers of clothing made of natural fibres such as cotton and wool provide more insulation than manmade ones. Do they have warm coats, hats and gloves and thick socks to wear?

If your outdoor session is going to be on a wet day you will need to ensure that waterproof outer clothing and footwear are worn. Whereas sessions on a sweltering day will require suitable clothing that will keep them cool but still protect them from scratches and stings that happen when outside. Long sleeves and trousers are a good idea. Sturdy shoes, trainers or wellies will protect feet from prickles or stings. Ensure that participants are wearing sun cream and a hat with a brim which covers the head and neck to help prevent sunburn. Communicate to parents the importance of appropriate clothing for extended periods by displaying images of children dressed in layers with long sleeves and trousers or even a child-sized mannequin wearing the type clothes suitable for being outdoors so that parents can see exactly the types of clothing which are suitable for your sessions.

When checking clothing also make sure that the adults are also appropriately dressed. Some schools and Early Years settings supply coats and waterproof trousers for staff and visitors. An uncomfortable adult will not give their best or want to participate for an extended period outdoors if they are wet or cold.

When getting ready to go outside it is fabulous if you have somewhere for children or young people to store and change in and out of their outdoor clothing. For boot storage in the cloakroom, shoe racks and clothes pegs with names or shoe sizes on to hold boots together when stored works well. Another great idea especially if your storage area is away from your changing area is to have a plank with 2 holes drilled either end. Thread rope for handles and sink holes along the length of the plank at intervals and insert doweling rods about 10 cms long and inverted the welly boots onto the sticks to allow them to dry after sessions.

If buying children or young people outdoor clothes is problematic for your budget, set up an 'outgrown' collection point for waterproofs and boots. Many parents are happy to pass these forward if asked. Jumble sales and charity shops are also good places to buy outdoor clothing for reasonable prices. Some major shops have also been known to donate waterproofs, so it may be worth being a bit cheeky and asking.

Weather Conditions

Before going outside check the local weather forecast. The BBC local weather app for the UK is great and gives an hourly forecast including wind speed. If you are in a different country, please look up your local weather station. If it is windy (above force 4) do not enter a woodland area especially if tree branches are moving at 20 degrees or more. When the weather has been wet or in times of extended drought there is an increased risk of tree limbs dropping suddenly although this can happen under any circumstances. This is a very common feature of Beech trees! Check children's' clothing before going outside that they are adequately dressed for the weather. Carry spare clothes including gloves and hats. I have several pack macs which can be put over the top of what the child is already wearing to reduce wind chill. An emergency shelter is great for putting a whole group of children in in case of being caught outside in harsh weather.

Ensure that children are suitably dressed in hot weather. Long sleeves and trousers will protect arms and legs from scratches and stings. Use hats and sun cream accordingly and set up shade protection as needed in your area.

Tree Climbing

Firstly, check with your insurance provider about whether they will cover you for this activity. Tree climbing is something which many adults are nervous about letting children try. It is an important skill and lets children try out their own abilities, calculate risks, test their strength and practice resilience. To comply with the limitations placed on us by insurance companies, an acceptable level of tree climbing is to the head height of the child or young person. I ask the children to make sure they have a friend of similar height to them standing by the tree they wish to climb. The child is then allowed to climb up to the height of the other persons head which is easily judged by their friend. This allows the children to support each other and give encouragement as well as practical advice and another set of eyes. Practicing climbing trees as well as coming back down again is a skill that the benefits outstrip the risk involved.

Lyme Disease

Lyme disease is caused by being bitten by an infected tick which first shows as a rash spreading out from the bite site. Untreated bites can spread the infection to other parts of the body and may develop into Lyme Disease which can cause serious symptoms affecting the skin, joint, nerves and heart.

Ticks do not jump or fly but climb on to passing humans from long grass or foliage. They are tiny insect like creatures about the size of a pinhead. Please note that most ticks in the UK are not infected by the bacterium that causes Lyme Disease, so most tick bites will not cause Lyme disease but because of the serious outcome of catching Lyme Disease, it is prudent to take precautions to prevent it.

Ticks are small and often you cannot feel them biting you. They cling onto the skin and feed by sucking the blood. Once they are engorged which can take up to 24–48 hours, the bacteria in the tick's gut travels up to their mouth and pass into the human. If you check regularly for ticks and remove them within 24 hours of being bitten you are less likely to develop Lyme Disease even if the tick was infected. A course of antibiotic medication will usually clear the infection. Seek medical attention as required.

Remove any ticks by gently gripping the tick as close to the skin as you can with fine tweezers or a tick removal devise and pull upwards, away from the skin being careful not to squeeze or crush it. Clean the skin with soap and water or disinfectant and wash your hands

Do not attempt to remove the tick by burning it off, smother it using petroleum jelly etc, squeeze it or pull it off using fingers.

Camp Fires

When you plan to have a campfire at your sessions there are many factors you will need to take into consideration. First, assess your area. If it is a very dry day and you have not had rain for quite a while or there are high winds seriously reconsider your plan to light a fire. If it is in a coniferous woodland or has peaty soil, there is a risk that the ground can smoulder unseen after a fire and reignite at a later point. If you do decide to have a fire I would recommend a raised fire pit and soak the ground below it with water first.

If the ground is suitable you can prepare by clearing away any leaf litter, so you are at the soil layer. If it is dry, soak it first. Avoid positioning your fire near overhanging trees and tree roots, making sure there is at least 4 metres gap from any shelters and 1.5 metres from seating.

Always have a reliable adult attend the fire even when children are doing other activities away from the area. Keep a bucket of water next to the fire. It can be used to plunge hands into or douse the fire. I like to put an old towel in it to soak to use as a fire blanket if needed. Make sure you always have sufficient water to extinguish the fire. Always keep a first aid kit to hand

I have welders gloves available for lifting kettles and pans off the fire. Make sure that long hair is tied back, and that fleeces, manmade fibres and loose clothing are not worn around the fire. (Cotton and wool are much less flammable)

Set up a visual barrier around the fire area that children may not enter when near the fire unless doing a specific fire activity. I use a white rope which is clearly seen and train children and young people how to behave in the fire area to ensure their safety.

Ensuring your session runs smoothly

Before setting out make sure that you have all the resources needed to complete each planned activity and include extras in case any of the adults want to be included or there is unsalvageable damage done during the process.

I find that it is sensible to over prepare and plan a spare activity just in case the planned session does not work as well as you wished, the children lose interest or it takes less time than you had anticipated. This could be games or activities which do not require any resources. If you do not need to use it during the session do not worry, you are prepared for next time. The main thing about planning for a session outside is to prepare to be flexible. Be prepared to change your session plan to fit in with the needs of the group or unexpected changes in the weather. Outdoor learning is sometimes unpredictable but can take you into new learning opportunities for both your group and yourself. If the weather changes unexpectedly and the ground becomes wet perhaps the running game planned could become more hazardous in slippery conditions or doing fire or very physical activities in very hot weather could be uncomfortable.

When thinking about the type of activities you would like to facilitate for the group consider the dynamics of the group. Do they need to gel as a group? Do they need to build their confidence outdoors, do they need activities which they can · extend into further play? What are their interests? Can you extend things they have learned in the classroom to the outdoors to approach the subject from a different angle to give them a deeper understanding? Can you encourage play that will become writing or talking prompts for when they return to the classroom?

Think of your sessions as a holistic way to complement what the child already knows, is interested in and their future learning. Make sure that when you are extending children's knowledge that you cover learning for all types of learners and have a multifaceted approach embracing learning styles. et children work together and scaffold each other's learning and understanding, let them problem solve and try out their own ideas and take control of their own experiences. Give them the opportunity to practice new skills to consolidate their own learning and build and test their own schemas. It will encourage resilience and make them more adaptable to changing mindsets in the face of new evidence, coping with failure and be willing to try out diverse ways to achieve which will carry them well into all stages of their lives. Celebrate their achievements when they succeed and encourage them to think of innovative approaches when they are dissatisfied with their results. Be their guide, their facilitator and their mentor but above all be the person who allows them to be themselves and celebrated their differences and ambitions. Embrace the opportunity to learn from them and develop your own practice.

Always be open to the needs of the group and where possible follow their lead. The best sessions I have ever encountered have been those that the children plan and led with very little adult input. They have not been those that have gone to plan but deviated at a tangent and embraced learning opportunities as they presented themselves. If your planned activity never makes it out of your bag because the children have been totally engaged in their own agenda, playing, cooperating and extending their own and each other's learning, that is a successful session.

A good outdoor session comprises of a mixture of child led learning, free play and building on the skills and addressing challenges that children have encountered in previous sessions. If possible at the end of each session, ask the children to feedback what they have learnt and achieved and if they would like to expand that the following session. Provide activities to support the interests and talents of the group.

Always remember that the most memorable sessions are those filled with laughter ... usually when things do not go to plan!

2

Games

Stalker

Preparation needed: none

Resources: none

Age range: primary, secondary, adult

Group size: any

Additional issues: none

Show the children how to stalk wildlife by walking quietly trying not to rustle their clothing and even keeping their breathing quiet so as not to alert wildlife that they are in the area. When everybody has practiced this spread the group around the area. Chose several stalkers and ask everybody else to close their eyes.

The stalkers need to move around as silently as they can and stand close to a person with their eyes closed and touch them on the head. If they are touched on the head by the stalker they open their eyes and sit down. They are now out of the game.

If they however hear the stalker or sense their presence they can say is the stalker standing beside me? If the stalker is there, then the stalker touches them on the head and they open their eyes. If, however the stalker is not near them and they ask the question they open their eyes and sit down, and they too are out of the game. The game finishes when everybody is either sitting on the ground or is now a stalker. A great game for raising awareness of movement and slight noise and that it can make wildlife scatter if they are making too much noise when trying to observe it. With younger children encourage them to change their body shape and move in a way which will confuse the wildlife and they wont think they are humans so slithering like a snake, making hands into antlers, scurrying like a squirrel is lovely to watch.

What are we learning from this activity?
How to walk quietly, how to listen carefully, how to challenge when you feel you are right, awareness of sounds in the environment.

Secret Stone

Preparation needed: none

Resources: none

Age range: primary, secondary, adult

Group size: any but works well with very large groups

Additional issues: make sure that boundaries of the game are outlined at the start. This game works well on playing fields, playgrounds, woodlands and beaches

This game is great fun and is good as a physical way to warm up on a chilly day. Divide the group equally into two teams. The team has a finish line, maybe between 2 trees or the fence posts at least 5 metres long. If there are no obvious landmarks, use a couple of ropes to define the finish lines. Give an object (and this could be anything which can be held in the closed palm of your hand for instance a pebble, a seashell, a button or a leaf, whatever you have to hand) to one member of one of the teams. Do not let the other team see who you pass the object too. The team can decide amongst themselves who will carry the secret stone but once that person has it they cannot swap it amongst themselves. Everyone in that team clenches their fist. The object of the game is to get the object to the other team's line without being caught. The team need to run and dodge their way to the other team's line. If they are tagged they must open their clenched hand to show they are not carrying the stone and play continues. If the person carrying the stone is tagged the game stops, everybody goes back to their team line and the second team are given possession of the stone. If the stone carrier manages to reach the other teams line, then a 'goal' is awarded to that team.

What are we learning from this activity?
Team work, gross motor skills, running, chasing, dodging and catching. Working out strategies with team mates to achieve a goal.

Scarf Tag

Preparation needed: bring bandanas or scarves

Resources: bandanas or scarves

Age range: primary, secondary, adult

Group size: any but works very well with large groups

Additional issues: watch out for trip hazards

Establish the boundaries of the game (how far the players can go) Each player needs to hold a scarf or bandana in their hand. If you do not have access to enough of these, you can use strips of ribbon or material instead. Chose a couple of chasers (They do not need a scarf.) All the other players need to avoid getting caught. When the chaser catches another player by touching them, the caught person and the catcher hold the scarf between them in their hands and run together to catch another person. The chasers, when there are 4 people in a chaser group all joined together, can split into pairs or stay joined together. The game continues until all players have been caught. The taggers can work out strategies to trap runners by working together as mini teams to corner them. Team work gives better results as a pair running together will be slower than an individual running.

What are we learning from this activity?
Working out strategies, negotiation, team work, gross motor skills, running, being aware of the needs and abilities of others. Making group decisions.

Grid Race

Preparation needed: this is a great game for playing on the beach

Resources: none

Age range: early years, primary, secondary, adult

Group size: any

Additional issues: none

Draw a grid in the sand on the beach making 1 square about 50 cm x 50 cms for each person playing that looks like a ladder.

Have an adult standing about 10-20 metres away. Everybody needs to stand in a square. When the leader shouts 'Grid Race' everybody must leave their square, run up the beach and go around the adult (or any other suitable marker) and race back to the grid and stand in a square.

Meanwhile, while the players are running, the leader needs to erase one or two squares from the end of the 'ladder'. When the players get back to the grid, those without a square are out of the game. Continue until there is only one square left. The player in the last square is the winner.

If you would like to play this game on school grounds, we have played it by drawing a chalk grid on the playground and putting a bean bag in each of the squares that are not in play. In the woodland we have played this game with sit mats making up the grid removing a few each time. (Do not do this on a wet day or the sit mats will become very muddy!).

What are we learning from this activity?
Running, racing, competition, gross motor skills, exercise, losing gracefully, cheering on others.

Roosting Starlings

Preparation needed: none

Resources: none

Age range: primary, secondary, adult

Group size: any

Additional issues: none

My favourite bird is probably the humble starling with their oily black plumage and its ability to work with other members of its flock to form a murmuration. The birds move together like a cloud swooping and sweeping over the sky to evade predators and establish group bonds. Talk to the children about the way they move and work together.

This is a two-part game; the first part is to form a murmuration when everybody works together following the movements of the others to form a synchronised pattern of moving as a team. Move around the available space together and shadow the movements of the people standing closest to you and move cooperatively as a team. This is harder than it sounds and is an activity which improves with practice.

When the group is working cooperatively, the leader shouts out "Roosting Starlings" each person must find a partner and one of the pair kneels on one knee with their other leg making the branch. The 'Starling' then needs to sit on the outstretched knee. The last pair to get themselves organised or any 'Starling' who does not have a roost will be out of the game. If you are working with younger children or a group who would not be comfortable with this have one person kneel and the starling should put their hands on the 'roosts' shoulder.

What are we learning from this activity?
Working with others, team work, cooperation. Learning about starlings and murmurations.

Water Trails

Preparation needed: gather resources

Resources: several empty washing up bottles or drink bottles with sports caps also work well, water

Age range: early years, primary, secondary, adult

Group size: small

Additional issues: watch out for trip hazards. This needs to be played on a dry day but not too hot or the water trail will evaporate too quickly

Chose a sure-footed runner or adult to lay the trail. Armed with squeezy bottles filled with water leave a water trail as you run by steadily squeezing the bottle allowing the water to come out. You will need to have mud paths or reasonable clear forest floor to do this as it would be much harder to follow a water trail over grass, but tree trunks could be splashed with water if there is no clear floor. When a bottle becomes empty change it for a full one and continue leaving the trail. When the trail layer has run out of water hide in the immediate vicinity of the last of the water trail and wait.

Count to 20 and let the others follow the trail until they catch up with or find the trail layer hiding.

What are we learning from this activity?
Speed, agility, running in rough terrain, following a trail, working with others. Hiding and seeking.

Jelly Fish Tag

Preparation needed: none

Resources: none

Age range: primary, secondary, adult

Group size: any but works well with large groups

Additional issues: ensure that the ground is reasonably clear of trip hazards. Set boundaries for the game. Works great on a beach to raise awareness of jellyfish stings

Jellyfish are invertebrates which have been around for millions of years. They can range in size from 2cms to 2m. some are clear, but others are bright colours or can produce their own light (bioluminescent).

Jelly fish have a mouth in the centre of its smooth, bag like body. It both eats and discards waste from its mouth and can squirt jets of water from it to propel itself forward at a speed of 8 km/h. It has no hearts, brains or eyes but their tentacles can sting their prey with their tentacles to stun them. Jellyfish stings can be painful for humans and in some cases can be fatal. Most stings occur when people accidently touch a jellyfish. Jellyfish eat fish, crabs, shrimps and other jelly fish which they digest very quickly so they can still float.

Jellyfish digest their food, which consists of fish, shrimp, crabs and tiny plants, very quickly. If they didn't, they wouldn't be able to float, being weighed down by the large, undigested grub in their body.

Select a few people to be the Jelly Fish. Everybody else will be little fishes swimming in the sea. Define the boundaries of the 'water' that the fish have to stay in. The jelly fish can try to touch the fish by moving around. If someone is touched by a Jelly Fish, they must place their hand on the place that was 'stung' For example is someone was 'stung' on the shoulder they need to put their hand on their shoulder. If they are 'stung' again but this time on the knee, they need to put their other hand on their knee. If they are tagged a third time they become a Jelly Fish too. Continue until the last person joins the Jelly Fish team. The jelly fish will learn that it is better to touch a part of a fish which will make it more difficult for them to get away easily.

What are we learning from this activity?
Following the rules of a game, working out strategies, working with others.

Ding Dong

Preparation needed: gather resources

Resources: a bell, string, a blindfold

Age range: early years, primary, secondary, adult

Group size: any

Additional issues: none

This is a great game to focus children to listen well and to also use careful movements rather than rushing to succeed at a task. This activity works well when used as an introduction to the Stalking game.

Tie a bell or cluster of bells onto a piece of string. Check in your music box for some bells, many habdasherers or craft shops will have one or alternatively the bells attached to chocolate rabbits or reindeers at seasonal times of the year.

Ask everyone to stand in a circle. Choose one person to be the listener and blindfold them. Stand them in the middle of the circle. The group need to pass the bell around the circle. If the blind folded person hears the bell they must point to where they heard it ring. The person holding the bell then becomes the next listener.

What are we learning from this activity?
Listening, focusing, moving slowly and in a controlled manner, cooperating with others.

Flora or Fauna Pop

Preparation needed: none

Resources: none

Age range: primary, secondary, adult

Group size: any

Additional issues: none

This is a great game for around the camp fire. Chose a category depending on what you have been or will be covering in your sessions. The categories could be Birds, Animals, Insects and minibeasts, plants, fish etc. To make it easier for younger children you may want to include all categories, to make it harder you may want to split the categories further for example British mammals, flying insects or you may want to introduce categories such as animals which hibernate, carnivores, those who lay eggs etc.

When everybody is sitting in a circle hold hands and the first person states the category being used. For example, 'Birds' taking it turns everybody has to say the name of a bird ... it might go like this, Robin, Kestrel, Swan, Song Thrush, Blue tit, Mallard Duck, Buzzard, then the next person may say um ... and not be able to think of a bird or repeat a bird previously said. If this occurs the group let go of hands and throws them into the air shouting 'POP!'

For older children and adults allow 5 seconds until 'pop', for younger children allow 10 or 20 seconds thinking time or allow the other children to offer suggestions.

Keep the list going until 'Pop' then the next person in the circle choses the next category.

What are we learning from this activity?
Categorising flora and fauna, fast thinking.

Changes

Preparation needed: none

Resources: none

Age range: early Years, primary, secondary, adult

Group size: any

Additional issues: none

This is a great game to help develop observational skills and memory. Divide the group into 2 groups. It works well with 5-10 people in each group so if you have a large class you may want more groups each taking a turn.

Ask the observation group to closely look at the other group of players (changers). Ask the observation group to turn away while the changer group changes 10 things about themselves. This could be things like swapping coats, taking off a hat, tying a scarf around their waist instead of their neck, changing hairstyle or swapping wellies. When they have completed this task ask the observation group to turn around and see if they can spot the 10 changes. When they have tried to guess ask the change group to reveal any unnoticed changes then swap groups, so the other group can make the changes.

The winning group is the most observant with one point for every change noticed. If you have multiple groups, the overall winner will be the team with the most points after observing all the other groups. When working with multiple groups it is a good idea for the teams to write down the changes, so they can be verified before points are awarded.

With younger groups you may want to simplify the activity by asking them to look at two people then make some changes and see if they can observe them.

What are we learning from this activity?
Observation, noticing differences, working with others, teamwork.

Marshmallow stick game

Preparation needed: gather resources

Resources: loppers, willow sticks no more than 1 cm in diameter and at least 40 cms long. A bag of marsh mallows. String or rope

Age range: early years, primary, secondary, adult

Group size: work in pairs

Additional issues: simplify for younger children. Keep the course reasonably simple

Make a simple assault course that 2 people can complete when joined together. Use string or rope between trees to step over or go under.

For very young children ask them to hold one stick between them and without letting go work their way to the end of the course.

For older children cut two straight sticks at least 40 cms long. Willow and hazel coppice poles work well for this. Lopper the ends so they are straight and blunt like the ends of a cylinder. Push a marshmallow onto both ends of each stick.

Two people need to stand facing each other. Raise their hands so their palms are facing each other and place the marshmallows on sticks in the centre of each palm so that each person is supporting both sticks between them with just their palms. The pair then need to move cooperatively to complete the course that has been set out without dropping either stick.

For Secondary and adults this activity can be made more difficult by introducing a third stick prepared the same way as the palm sticks with marshmallows at either end but this time the third stick is supported by the players foreheads which means that they cannot look down and plan their route so easily. If you can pair people of similar heights it helps.

What are we learning from this activity?
Cooperation, communication, working with others, shadowing movements, balancing.

Lizard Tails

Preparation needed: none

Resources: a scarf or length of material for each group

Age range: early years, primary, secondary, adult

Group size: large or medium

Additional issues: simplify for younger children

The common lizard can be found in the UK and Europe. It is a viviparous lizard which means it has live young rather than laying eggs. Common lizards hibernate from November until March. They eat spiders, insects, snails and earthworms.

You might see common lizards basking in the sun on heathlands, moorlands, grasslands and woodlands. Animals which like to eat lizards (predators) are foxes, domestic cats, hawks, crows and jays They can shed their tail as a defence mechanism when they are attacked and grow a new tail which is often shorter and darker than the original.

To play Lizard tails split the group into smaller groups of about 4-6 children. They need to stand in a row and place their hands on the waist of the person in front of them. They are not allowed to let go for the duration of the game. If they do the front of the group has to stop and wait for the rest of the group to re-join them. The last person in each group needs to have a scarf or piece of material tucked into their waist band. Moving together as a team, the object of the game is for the 'head' of each lizard to capture the tail of the other lizard(s).

The winner is the lizard which captures the tail of another lizard. If you want to extend the game the tailless lizard needs to go to the leader and regenerate another tail (tuck another scarf into the waistband of the last person in the team. The winner would then be the lizard with the most tails at the end of the game.

What are we learning from this activity?
Team work, moving together, coordination, gross motor, learning about lizard facts.

Frogs and Butterflies

Preparation needed: print and laminate cards with a picture of a frog on one side and a picture of a butterfly on the other

Resources: laminated cards (at least one per member of the group and maybe 5 more)

Age range: early years, primary, secondary, adult

Group size: work in two teams. This works well with teams of about 5 to 10

Additional issues: you can use any pictures, frogs and butterflies is just an example. You may want to use distinct types of leaves like oak and ash or mammals verses reptiles depending on what your group focus is

Have at least 25 laminated cards with pictures of a frog on one side and a butterfly on the other side. If you have a large group you will need more cards, several more than the total number of players works the best, but have an odd number.

Place half of the sheets on the ground Butterfly side facing up and half of the sheets Frog side up. Spread them out over a wide area. The sheets are not to move location during the game.

Split the group into two groups. One group will be the Frog team and the other group will be the butterfly team.

Each team needs to flip the cards to show their team emblem within a set time (2-3 minutes works well.) The rules should include that nobody can touch a card if another person is touching it, but you can only touch a card for the time it takes to flip it. You may not touch someone in the opposite group (no rugby tackles!)

When the time is up count how many of each type of emblem is facing upwards. The team with the most is the winner.

If you want to make the game more challenging have a base that each team member must return to the starting point before flipping another card. Alternatively, this can also be done as a relay with only one 'flipper' from each team at a time. They must flip a card then return to base before the next team member can go.

What are we learning from this activity?
This game is good for encouraging physical activity, team work, agility and speed.

Human Kaleidoscope

Preparation needed: none

Resources: loppers, gather straight sticks of similar length and width at least 40 cms long. Coloured wool or thread if desired

Age range: primary, secondary, adult

Group size: works well in groups of 4 to 8

Additional issues: simplify for younger children

This works well to develop concentration and mindfulness. Gather 2 straight sticks per person of similar length and width at least 40 cms long. Trim with loppers if necessary so all the sticks are of comparable size. If you would like a colourful kaleidoscope you can decorate the sticks using coloured wool, ribbon, strips of cloth or thread by winding it around each stick to cover the bark.

When everybody has two sticks stand in a circle facing each other. Start with all the sticks pointing into the centre of the circle. Everybody needs to synchronise their movements and it works best if somebody takes the lead role and everybody else follows. Slowly take a step backwards and each person points their sticks towards their other stick to form a triangle. Now point the sticks away from each other so they form a point with the stick of the person standing next to you, cross the sticks and join the end of the stick with that of the person one place away from you. Experiment as a group to find different combinations. Take it in turns to lead and learn from each other. With a little bit of practice and group coordination this activity looks amazing. Remember to keep movements slow and synchronised for the best result.

What are we learning from this activity?
Cooperation, communication, working with others, shadowing movements and working as part of a team.

Heads or Tails

Preparation needed: none

Resources: a coin, a tree cookie or a flat stone with a picture of a head on one side and a tail on the other

Age range: early years, primary, secondary, adult

Group size: work with any sized groups

Additional issues: for early years no one is out! If it is a damp day make sit mats available for anybody not wearing waterproof trousers

I love this game and it is such a simple 5-minute filler which everybody loves to play. Everybody needs to stand and put their hands on either their head or on their tail (their bottom).

Flip a coin and shout out which side the coin lands on: If the coin lands on heads, everyone with their hands on their heads loses and must kneel on one knee however if it lands on tails, everyone with their hands on their tail must go on one knee.

Everybody can then change their hands to the head or tail position before the next toss of the coin. If someone loses again then they must kneel on two knees, the next time they must sit on the ground and may no longer play. If someone loses the first time and is on one knee, if they win the second time they may stand up again.

I often play this with a double-sided sit mat which has a different colour on either side making it easier for the children to see the result.

What are we learning from this activity?
Listening to instructions, participating in a game, learning to lose gracefully, random chance.

Peg Tag

Preparation needed: bring a packet of clothes pegs and give a couple of pegs to each person

Resources: clothes pegs, 2 or 3 per person

Age range: early years, primary, secondary, adult

Group size: any

Additional issues: for smaller children demonstrate how to use pegs and attach them to clothing prior to play (pegs are great for developing finger muscles ready for writing!)

Everybody has a couple of clothes pegs attached to their clothes. During their course of the session the idea of the game is to secretly attach their pegs into other people without them realising. If you find a peg attached to your clothes at any time you will need to try and secretly attach it to someone else. If someone catches you trying to pin a peg in them you must put the peg back on yourself and try again later. At the end of the session the leader will ask everybody to search themselves for pegs. They may need a partner to assist them in this. Any people without any pegs attached to them at the close of the session are the winners. You may like to ask each person to decorate their pegs with their name (felt tips work well on wooden pegs or little stickers on plastic pegs) and extra stealth kudos could be awarded for the players to return the peg to the owner without them noticing.

For younger children ask them to attach the pegs to the accompanying adults without being noticed. The adults can then 'not find them' to ensure everybody achieves success.

What are we learning from this activity?
Team work, stealth, stalking, moving quietly, keep movements close.

Water Duelling

Preparation needed: gather resources, play on a sweltering day or when suitably dressed in waterproofs

Resources: 2 buckets, 2 sticks (about half a metre long) water, 2 face cloths, 2 sit mats

Age range: early years, primary, secondary, adult

Group size: any size, split the group into 2 teams

Additional issues: as this game involves the potential for getting wet, it may be better to make it optional or give children who are reluctant the chance to play another role as a referee or score keeper. This is a great summer game especially on the beach or school grounds. It could be part of an alternative sports day

Divide the group into 2 teams. Each team has a bucket of water, a long stick and a handkerchief sized piece of material (I find a bandana or face cloths work really well) and a sit mat.

The first person from each team stands on the sit mat. During play they may not step off the mat, if they do the other team scores a point. The sit mats need to be positioned about 3-5 meters apart (depending on the height of the players.

The bucket of water is placed in front of the players. The face cloth is submerged in the bucket. Pick up the soggy cloth with the stick and in the manner of casting a fishing rod, throw it at your opponent. If you hit the other person on any part of the body you score 2 points. The other person may duck or move but if they step off the mat the other team is awarded a point. Both players must stand on their mats until both cloths have been thrown. Points are awarded by the referees and then the next players take their positions on the sit mats. The winning team will hold the most points after each team member has participated in the agreed number of duels, usually 1–3.

What are we learning from this activity?
Being part of a team, encouraging others, a sense of fun, throwing skills and accuracy.

Welly Throwing

Preparation needed: gather together resources

Resources: welly boots, rope, stones (one for each player), chalk, rope as a starting line

Age range: early years, primary, secondary, adult

Group size: any

Additional issues: make sure that children stand well away from the throwing area in case of any stray wellies. If you have several wellies available, make sure that everybody stays behind the line until they have all been thrown before venturing out to mark the spot

Ask each player to select a stone and decorate it with their name or other distinguishing marks. Stand at the starting line and throw a welly boot as far as you can. Mark the spot where the welly lands with your pebble and return the welly boot to the starting line ready for the next persons turn. The winner will be the person who has managed to throw their welly the furthest.

What are we learning from this activity?
Choosing and creating a marking stone, mark making, gross motor, fine motor, developing throwing skills, comparing.

Skittle Dangle

Preparation needed: throw a rope over a tree branch which is well away from the trunk of the tree. Make sure there is enough room under the tree for the group to make a circle. Tie a light ruck sack or a coat made into a bundle to the end of the rope. A large blow up beach ball also works well

Resources: rope, a light ruck sack or coat

Age range: primary, secondary, adult

Group size: up to about 20

Additional issues: ensure that all players are willing participants

This is a very silly game where the participants are human skittles. Stand the players in a circle around the rope pendulum. One person swings the rope in a circular motion. Any person (skittle) who is touched by the ball however lightly needs to (dramatically) fall over. Any people still standing at the end of the swing can be knocked over with subsequent swings. At the end of the round the players or a referee award points to the best skittle tumble. That person then becomes the rope swinger in the next round. This is a game which is great for fun and frivolity. This game can also be played on a school playing field where there are goal posts available (without a net).

If you throw a rope over a branch but it is not where you want it to be you can move it along the branch by holding the end of the rope in your hand and using your wrist throw a loop (like you were casting a little fishing rod). By directing the loop to the left or the right you can position the rope in the correct position.

What are we learning from this activity?
Joining in with others, a sense of fun, dramatic and acting skills.

Tug of War

Preparation needed: chose an area free of trip hazards

Resources: a rope, 2 ribbons or some string

Age range: early years, primary, secondary, adult

Group size: 6/20 depending on the length of your rope

Additional issues: make sure that the teams are evenly matched not just in numbers but also height and weight

Find an area clear of trip hazards. Draw or mark out 2 lines on the ground. Tie a ribbon or rag onto the centre of the rope. Divide the group into 2 teams. Each team stands at either end of the rope. Everybody needs to hold onto the rope with both hands. On the signal from the referee both teams need to pull on the rope. The team which gains the most ground wins the Tug of War. The ribbon passing the line on the ground can assist the referee in making that decision. The team needs to work cooperatively with each other and devise a team strategy to achieve their goal.

What are we learning from this activity?
Working with others, being part of a team, needing others to achieve a goal.

Reflection Relay

Preparation needed: gather resources. Chose an area free of trip hazards

Resources: a mirror/ mirror card or cd for each team

Age range: early years, primary, secondary, adult

Group size: any, divide into teams of up to 5-10

Additional issues: make sure the area is reasonably clear of trip hazards

This is a fun team game which is great for an alternative sports day or as a game for any session.

Chose an area clear of trip hazards. Divide the groups into teams and give each team a mirror. I have some safety mirrors mounted onto wood for this game. Stand a person or have a tree or post about 20 or so metres away from the teams. The first member of each team needs to walk backwards towards the marker at the end of the course. They may only use their mirror and verbal encouragement from team members to direct them. They need to walk around the person at the end of the course and return, still walking backwards to their team and give the mirror to the next person and so on until all members of the team have completed the course. The winning team will be the first team to complete the mission.

What are we learning from this activity?
The properties of mirrors and reflections, moving backwards, working as a team, coordination, left and right and realising it is different when giving instructions to someone who is facing you, encouraging others.

Pass the Pinecone

Preparation needed: none

Resources: a pinecone or any other object you may have to hand

Age range: early years, primary, secondary, adult

Group size: any

Additional issues: none

Stand the group in a circle quite close together with their hands behind their backs. Choose a person to stand in the middle of the circle. The person in the middle of the circle must close their eyes while the rest of the group chant 'Pass the pinecone, pass the pinecone' at the same time as passing the pine cone amongst themselves.

The guesser counts to 10 then opens their eyes. The rest of the group continues passing the pinecone amongst themselves behind their backs. The guesser then has 3 chances to find out who is holding the pinecone by pointing at a person. The person being pointed at must reveal their hands. If they are holding the pinecone then they swap places with the guesser in the entre of the circle and the game starts again. If after 3 guesses the pinecone is not found, the person holding the pine cone is chosen to take the place of the guesser.

You can use any object you have to hand to play this game. I often use a squirrel puppet as I always seem to have them in my bag and aptly rename the game pass the squirrel. You can make the game more complex by having several objects being passed at the same time.

What are we learning from this activity?
Team work, cooperation and looking for body language and facial clues to guess who has the object.

Sticky Spiders Web

Preparation needed: gather resources

Resources: alder cones, coloured wool, masking tape, newspaper if alder cones are not available

Age range: early years, primary, secondary, adult

Group size: small or have several spider's webs

Additional issues: make sure you remove everything at the end of the game

Spider Facts: There are approximately 40,000 different species of spiders around the world ranging from one that is less than 1mm long (the Patu marplesi) to a Goliath tarantula with a leg span of up to 28 cms and is big enough to catch birds. They are arthropods and have an exoskeleton. All spiders have 8 legs and are in the class of arachnid. They also have 8 eyes. Most spiders are carnivorous and eat other insects and animals. They make webs and egg sacs from spider silk which they make in their spinneret glands in their abdomens. Spiders silk is very strong and is the strongest fibre known to man, 5 times as strong as steel. Some spiders create webs which can take them about an hour to do to catch prey, some spiders use their silk to carry them in the wind to find a new home, this is called ballooning.

When making a web, a spider will climb to a high point and release a thread hoping that the wind will blow it to attach on to another point. The spider them pulls the thread taut. This is known as the bridge. It then creates a Y shape underneath the bridge and makes some radius threads and then adds in a sticky spiral thread for catching insects. The spider can detect when something is caught in its web by vibrations.

Using masking tape (paper sticky tape) construct a spider's web between 2 trees or fixed points. Make sure that the sticky side of the tape is all facing in one direction. Each player needs to select some alder cones and decorate them with coloured wool to represent bugs. If you do not have access to alder cones, small scrunched up newspaper balls also work well. It is easier if each person has their own colour to make identifying their bugs easier.

Decide on a standing point a metre or so away from the web (sticky side facing you) and take it in turns to throw the 'bugs' at the web. The winner is the person who manages to stick the most bugs to the web.

When you have finished the activity please remove all the tape from the trees and dispose of responsibly.

What are we learning from this activity?
Throwing skills, gross motor, aiming, making resources, learning facts about spiders and web construction. Designing a web structure.

Den, Fire, Log pile, Bushes and Friends

Preparation needed: none

Resources: none

Age range: early years, primary, secondary, adult

Group size: large

Additional issues: simplify for younger children by using less categories

Stand the players in a group. The leader will say either Den, fire, trees, bushes or friends.

If the instruction is 'Den' the players must get themselves into groups of 3 and one player crouches down while the other two join hands to form a roof for a shelter over the crouching player.

If the instruction is 'fire' then 4 players must stand facing each other with their arms raised to represent a fire.

When the leader calls out 'log pile' 5 players must form a group facing each other with their arms outstretched in front of them and overlaying their team mates to form a log pile.

When the instruction 'bushes' is called out 2 players need to crouch down next to each other to become bushes.

The instruction 'friends' requires the players to run around and high five (or shake hands) with as many people in the whole group as they can.

As the group learns the responses speed up the instructions. Any group doing the wrong formation, having the wrong number of people in their group or being the last to be organised will be out of the game and need to move to the edge and shout encouragement to the others. This is a good game to warm children up ready for further activities which require concentration or following instructions. It is also a great way to get children into groups for the next activity so if you need them to be in a group of 5 end the activity on 'log pile' or if you need pairs end on 'bushes'.

What are we learning from this activity?
Listening to instructions, following instructions, gross motor control, working with others cooperatively and getting organised quickly.

Grumpy Badger

Preparation needed: none

Resources: none

Age range: early years, primary, secondary, adult

Group size: large

Additional issues: none but if children don't like the idea of a Grumpy Badger you could always use something like 'Fluffy Bunny' instead

Sit everyone in a circle. This game is a great game for playing around the camp fire and causes lots of hilarity.

One person is chosen to be the answerer. Take it in turns to go around the circle and ask questions. The answer to every question must be 'Grumpy Badger' for example "What is your name?" "What do you like for tea?" "What are your socks made from?" "What is your teacher called?" If the answerer smiles, laughs or says something else apart from 'Grumpy Badger' the person asking the question becomes the new answerer. Everybody can fire questions at the grumpy badger to try to make them smile. If they manage to not smile or laugh for a minute, then they can chose a new grumpy badger to take their place.

What are we learning from this activity?
Keeping a straight face, developing a sense of humour, speaking and listening, asking questions. I have found that even the most reluctant talkers are keen to have a turn at asking a question.

The Circle of Trust

Preparation needed: none

Resources: none

Age range: primary, secondary, adult

Group size: any

Additional issues: do not play this game when wearing gloves as hands can slip easily

You need an even number of players for this to work well, it also helps if they are of similar body size so children who were in year one would not be able to hold the weight of those in year 6.

Everybody needs to stand in a circle. Give each child a number 1 or 2 alternating as you go around the circle. Everybody needs to hold hands. On your signal all the children who have the number 1 need to lean forward and all the children who are 2's need to lean backwards. Everybody needs to support each other and the whole circle requires the cooperation and trust of everybody else. When the group has balanced successfully bring them back upright and change roles where the 1's lean backwards and the 2's lean forward. To make this more challenging and to test their trust with each other try this with their eyes closes.

What are we learning from this activity?
Working with others to achieve a goal, teamwork, focus, meditation and mindfulness, learning to trust the other people in your group. Balance.

Giant Beetle Drive

Preparation needed: none

Resources: a dice. Natural resources

Age range: early years, primary, secondary, adult

Group size: small/medium. Working in small groups works well too

Discuss the anatomy of a beetle (or whichever creature is of interest to you at the time.)

Take it in turns to throw the dice and collect natural materials to build the beetle. You can make small individual beetles or a giant beetle as part of a team game.

If you throw a 1 it means you can collect material to make the head, a 2 for the thorax, 3 for the abdomen, 4 for legs (there are six of these) 5 for the antenna (there are 2) and 6 for the wings (2 hard outer wings which are called elytra with the 2 soft hind wings underneath).

The first group to complete their beetle is the winner.

What are we learning from this activity?
The anatomy of a beetle, turn taking, searching and collecting suitable materials, working as part of a team, building a large model.

Dotty Spotting

Preparation needed: place sticky dots with letters on around your outdoor area prior to the session

Resources: sticky dots, marker pen, postcards, pencils

Age range: primary, secondary, adult

Group size: any

Additional issues: it may help to give children cards already prepared with a dash for each letter, so they can see how many words there are and how many letters are in each word

Write a word or a saying on some sticky dots. Each dot should have a separate letter on it and place around your outdoor area before the session. During the session whenever the children spot a letter they need to write it down and once they have all or most of them they need to unscramble the letters to reveal the word or words. Make sure that the children know how many letter dots are placed around the area. The lettered dots could give a clue as to where a prize could be or a clue as to where the next activity is hidden.

What are we learning from this activity?
Observational skills, anagrams, letters, assisting others.

3

Activities not requiring tools

Bug Catching

Preparation needed: collect resources

Resources: umbrellas, collecting pots, magnifying glasses, bushes and hedgerows, id sheets or books, camera for recording finds

Age range: early years, primary, secondary, adult

Group size: any

Additional issues: be careful about touching insects and bugs as some (especially the hairy ones) as some cause skin irritation

Have you ever been on a bug hunt and not been able to find may bugs? Playgrounds can sometimes be quite sparse, but most schools have access to hedges, trees and bushes and this is a method of bug collecting that works well. Have your collecting pots or trays at the ready. Hold the open umbrella upside down under a bush, tree or hedge, shake the hedge or bush vigorously for about 20 seconds. Tip anything you find into your collecting pot and have a look at what you have caught. Use ID charts and books to identify what you have found. Check out www.naturedetectives.org.uk for simple id sheets, or look at ID charts from the fields studies council www.field-studies-council.org/publications.

When you have finished looking at the bugs you have found return them to the locations you found them.

What are we learning from this activity?
Respect for nature, habitats, mini beasts, observation, collecting and identifying.

Stone Stories

Preparation needed: collect and paint simple pictures onto smooth stones or pebbles, leave to dry. You may want to cover with varnish if you would like to reuse these as a resource

Resources: pebbles, a bag to keep them in, paints (acrylic paints, poster paints) varnish

Age range: early years, primary, secondary, adult

Group size: any

Additional issues: works well when used in a group and is excellent as a camp fire activity

You may want to prepare the stones before the session or with older children, they may want to paint one each.

On each stone paint a picture, keep it simple! Ideas could be a tree, a flower, a star, a fish, a river, a cloud, a leaf, a boy, a girl, a princess, a frog, a knight, an ogre, a hero, a king, a queen, a castle, a witch, a cat, a dog, a bird, a bear, a witch, a cave, an apple, a cake etc or anything else you can think of. You may want to theme your stones to incorporate your classroom themes. When the stones are dry you may want to varnish them to preserve the pictures. Put the stones in a bag and start telling a story. Each person takes it in turn to add to the story. They need to take a stone out of the bag and incorporate the picture in their tale. For beach school you could make a bag of stones with sea themed pictures. For little people paint different characters on the stones and order them to make a well-known story for instance 3 bears, goldilocks, bowls, chairs and beds and use them to help children sequence a story. For a themed day you may want the children to find stones that you have previously hidden around the site, bring them all together and try to guess the story for instance a mouse, a nut, a snake an owl and a fox could lead into a Gruffalo hunt.

What are we learning from this activity?
Turn taking, imagination, storytelling, sequencing, working with others.

Spiderweb Wands

Preparation needed: collect resources. Works best in the morning, preferably when there is still dew around

Resources: willow whip, string, a piece of card, spray bottle, water

Age range: early years, primary, secondary, adult

Group size: any

Additional issues: none

This activity works well in the morning when there has been an overnight dew. Carefully bend your willow rod into a loop about the diameter of a large grapefruit. Tie with string. Search your outdoor area, in bushes, the hedgerow, corners of play equipment etc until you find a spiderweb. Very carefully capture the web on the loop of your wand and let the group inspect it up close. If it is dry you may want to lightly spray it with a fine mist of water to make the web more pronounced. If the sun is out hold it above the sheet of card and look at the delicate shadow cast by the web.

Make a willow wand for each child and using string or wool to make the web. Decorate with grass and leaves.

What are we learning from this activity?
Observation skills, respect for nature, learning about spiders and webs, making and decorating a craft item.

Seed Bombing

Preparation needed: collect resources

Resources: compost or crumbly soil, wild flower/meadow flower seeds, a little cooking oil to bind, a bowl. If building catapults a range of sticks, string, scissors, elastic bands (old bicycle inner tyre tubes work well) or elastic

Age range: early years, primary, secondary, adult

Group size: any

Additional issues: check for any allergy issues when handling seeds

Mix together seeds, compost and soil and a little oil to bind the mixture together. Press into a ball the size of a marble or even bigger sized balls about the size of a golf ball depending on your launch method.

Use sling shots which you can make from forked sticks and elastic from haberdashery stores. Alternatively, you may want to have a throwing competition or build a catapult to launch the seed ball into your chosen area. Set the children a challenge to build a machine to launch their seed bombs.

The seed bombs will disintegrate on impact, disperse the seeds and encourage wild flowers to grow. It is better to seed bomb areas which are open, rather than deep shade, the edge of a playing field or woodland, flower beds etc will encourage insects and butterflies to your area.

What are we learning from this activity?
Encouraging butterfly friendly habitats, making resources, design and technology to 'launch' the seed bombs, a bit of guerrilla gardening.

Leaf Printing

Preparation needed: gather resources

Resources: paint, card, small rollers, paint tray

Age range: early years, primary, secondary, adult

Group size: any

Additional issues: do not use Holly leaves as they will not lay flat enough to do this activity

Find a selection of leaves. Varied sizes and shapes is ideal. With a small paint roller, carefully roll on a layer of paint onto the leaf and place face down onto paper or card. Press down and then carefully peel off the paper to leave the leaf print. Allow to dry. Why not cut them out and use them to make a wall display or collage. How about making red and orange prints to make a bonfire picture for the classroom. You can also use small leaves to print onto tree cookies, card to make greetings cards or if you use paint or ink suitable for material how about designing your own forest fashions. If you do t-shirts make sure you place a piece of card inside the t-shirt to ensure that the print does not soak through to the back.

This method also is very effective if using printing inks and rollers.

What are we learning from this activity?
Using natural materials to make art work. Printing and painting, scissor skills, individual contribution to a larger piece of art work. Fashion design.

Streamer Dancing

Preparation needed: gather resources

Resources: masking tape, scissors, crepe paper

Age range: early years, primary

Group size: any

Additional issues: you may want to pre-cut the crepe paper strips prior to the activity

Choose a stick which is comfortable for you to hold, at least the diameter of your thumb. Ask a friend to help you by holding up a strip of masking tape about 40 cms long. Chose a variety of colours of crepe paper. Cut strips about 5 cms wide and 40 cm long. Starting about 5 cms in from the masking tape, stick the end of the crepe paper strip to the masking tape. Add on another colour and continue until you are 5 cm from the other end of the masking tape. Wrap the masking tape around and around the end of the stick. Hold the other end of the stick and shake it.

Use as a dancing stick. Lovely for celebrating May day or exploring Morris dancing or country dancing with children. Small children take great delight running around with these streamer sticks on windy days, watching the streamers flutter behind them.

What are we learning from this activity?
Making our own resources. Looking at traditions and cultures. Exploring different genres of dance.

Felt Leaf Badges

Preparation needed: gather resources, collect leaves, identify

Resources: felt squares, leaves, camera, printer, square paper, pencils, scissors, glue, safety pins, leaf chart, tapestry needles, cotton or embroidery silks

Age range: early years, primary, secondary, adult

Group size: any

Additional issues: simplify for younger children

Leaves can be used in a wide range of activities in the outdoor classroom. They are a free and abundant resource. An activity can be to collect as many different shapes or colours that you can find or in autumn making leaf piles to jump in, there is nothing like an autumnal walk and walking through crunchy leaves. On a woodland or outdoor walk collect a variety of leaves. Can you support children to identify these leaves and chose their favourite? For the larger leaves, either draw around the leaves onto squared paper and reduce the size to a 'badge' sized leaf outline, or back in the classroom you can photograph or scan the leaves on a computer and reduce them or cut out a free hand leaf. Cut out the leaf pattern and use it as a stencil on a piece of felt. Draw around it and cut out a felt leaf shape. Try making felt leaves of assorted colours perhaps to show the range of autumnal colours. You can sew each leaf to represent the veins of the leaf and then arrange your finished leaves and either sew them into place or stick using glue. Mount the leaves onto either a button badge using glue or sew/glue on a safety pin to enable the badge to be worn. This activity makes a lovely present and makes a lovely activity to complete around the camp fire or under a tarpaulin in wet weather.

What are we learning from this activity?
Using nature as inspiration for craft activities, choosing and selecting, making an item, developing scissor skills, fine motor skills, sewing.

Leaf People

Preparation needed: none

Resources: leaves, white paper, pens, glue, scissors, if you wish to display these creations: laminator and pouches or clear sticky backed plastic

Age range: early years, primary

Group size: any

Additional issues: please be aware of hazards associated with using a laminator. Ensure that the leaves are dry especially if using glue before laminating or enclosing in plastic

Collect a range of leaves and arrange into 'people' or creature shapes. Use the different leaf shapes to be creative. When you are happy with your creation dab glue onto the leaves to hold them in place. Draw eyes onto white paper or stickers and attach. If you want to preserve your leaf person/ creature, laminate your creation to display and cut around the shape leaving a 5cm border. If you hole punch the top of the border you can hang them up. With lots of them you could create a mobile. How about making a leaf family? Link with literacy by using the people and leaf creatures for story telling or make all the characters in a story.

What are we learning from this activity?
Collecting and selecting, creativity, fine motor skills, language and literacy.

Shades of Leaves

Preparation needed: when in DIY or hardware shop collect a range of the colour paint charts, you can also make your own charts by mixing paints in leaf colours (greens, yellows, browns etc depending upon the time of year) and making them lighter or darker in graduated steps

Resources: paint charts

Age range: early years, primary, secondary, adult

Group size: any but have enough paint charts for everyone

Additional issues: if you make homemade paint charts it might be a clever idea to laminate them so that this resource can be used many times

Give the children a paint chart each and ask them to match as many of the shades on the chart with leaves and set them out as a spectrum. They will be amazed at the variety of shades of greens, yellows, oranges and browns in leaves.

If you would like to make this into a classroom display, give the children a sticky card blank made by cutting strips of card and sticking double sided sticky tape along the strip. (I prefer double sided carpet tape as it is strong even if the leaves are slightly damp) Stick the leaves or parts of the leaves on the strips and display alongside the original chart.

What are we learning from this activity?
Fine motor skills, personal artwork using natural resources, choosing and selecting resources, sequencing, fine motor, sorting, creative skills, Art, colours, shades and spectrums, selecting and matching.

Bug Stones

Preparation needed: collect resources. This activity works well in school grounds, woodlands and beaches

Resources: stones and pebbles, coloured chalks and charcoal

Age range: early years, primary, secondary, adult

Group size: any

Additional issues: take hand washing equipment or wet wipes with you as this is quite a messy activity

Collect a range of smooth stones or pebbles. If your area does not have any suitable stones, it is possible to buy a sack of pebbles in garden centres and DIY stores.

Decorate the stones with drawings of bugs and mini beasts. Using chalks and charcoal means that the colours will wash off if left outside in the rain (pastels will last longer than chalks and provide more vivid colours but are less environmentally friendly). Alternatively, you can wash the stones to make them reusable for other groups and occasions. Make a bug parade by arranging the bug stones in a line. Use them for counting, sorting, building mini dens homes, exploring habitats etc

You can try using several stones to make a minibeast, how about using small pebbles in a row to make a caterpillar or a round pebble balanced on top of a long stone to make a snail with its shell.

If on a beach, try drawing rock pool life on pebbles instead.

What are we learning from this activity?
Fine motor skills, using different mediums for mark making, personal artwork using natural resources, choosing and selecting resources, colours, minibeasts, seashore life, sorting, counting, arranging, building, habitats, the impermanency of natural art work.

Stone Faces

Preparation needed: gather resources. This activity works well in school grounds, woodlands and beaches

Resources: stones, chalks and charcoal sticks

Age range: early years, primary, secondary, adult

Group size: any

Additional issues: you will need hand washing facilities or wet wipes as this can be quite a messy activity

Make a face from stones and pebbles, if on the beach the addition of sea shells can be very effective. Balance small stones on top of larger ones to make a relief picture of a face, for example a large flattish stone or a boulder can be used as a face, Features can be added on by using other stones balanced on the first stone to create a 3D face. You can use chalks or charcoal to add in details such as pupils in the eyes, or nostrils on the nose or alternatively you can make the rule you can only use what you can find!

Talk to the children about facial features and how different emotions can change the features. Try making happy faces, surprised faces and angry faces. What bit of the face changes? Can they change or add stones to their stone to make the face have different emotions?

If you take a photograph with each face change you could make a Stop Motion Animation of the changing faces of stone back in the classroom.

What are we learning from this activity?
Fine motor skills, facial features, emotions and facial expressions, using different mediums for personal artwork using natural resources, choosing and selecting resources, colours, mark making, arranging, the impermanency of natural art work

Bell and Shell Shaker

Preparation needed: gather resources

Resources: a forked stick, wool, ribbon, string, bells and shells with holes in, scissors

Age range: early years, primary, secondary, adult

Group size: any

Additional issues: assistance maybe needed for younger children

Each person needs a forked stick Y shaped. Wind wool and ribbon around the prongs of the stick to make it beautiful and individual. Collect shells, especially ones with holes in it. You can make holes with awls or drills if careful. Thread on a string along with some bells (you can buy sets of small bells in the pound shops in the run up to Christmas, well worth stocking up on some!) Beer bottle tops can also work well if you drill through the centre of them. Tie the string between the prongs of the stick and shake.

What are we learning from this activity?
Making resources, making music, using a variety of materials to make different sounds. Tying and winding, threading and cutting.

Animal Prints

Preparation needed: print outs of animal footprints

Resources: container, water, paint brush

Age range: early years, primary

Group size: any

Additional issues: none

This is a dry day activity. Many websites, books and ID charts have pictures of wildlife foot prints. I like to laminate individual animal prints and give each child one or two to work with. Using a paintbrush or fingers, copy the shape of the animal foot print onto a flat surface (mud, tarmac, paving slabs) Can your friends identify which animal track you have made?

Now collect a range of natural materials such as mud, twigs and leaves and try making a relief animal foot print.

Which type of print making is easier to identify, which is easier to make? If you leave the water print for a while what happens to it?

What are we learning from this activity?
Identifying animal tracks, using varied materials and their properties. Temporary construction and leave no trace.

Gold Rush

Preparation needed: collect lots of little stones or pebbles, prepare the 'gold' in advance, distribute the 'gold' in your outdoor area

Resources: small stones or pebbles, gold, newspaper, buckets or pots, tin plates, water, sand, sieves

Age range: early years, primary, secondary, adult

Group size: any

Additional issues: make sure paint is nontoxic and encourage children to wash their hands after activity

Create a gold rush in your outdoor area. Wash and dry small stones and pebbles. Spray paint with gold paint and leave to dry. (metallic spray paint is available in DIY stores, car accessory shops and art and craft shops or online.

Put the gold pieces around your outdoor area and arm your children with collecting pots and let them find the pieces. This can be further extended by burying pieces of gold in a sand pit and giving children sieves to hunt for the gold.

How about a session panning for gold? Show the children how to scoop up a mixture of water, sand and gold bits onto a tin plate and using a swirling motion let the sand wash off until the heavier gold pieces are left behind.

If you also prepare stones painted with silver and copper, you could then extend the activity into sorting. These activities fit in well with mining, the American wild west, treasure hunts and can also be used for pirates, silver or gold anniversaries and celebrations.

What are we learning from this activity?
History, mining, precious metals, panning for gold, treasure hunting, gross motor and fine motor skills, observational skills, sorting and collecting.

Christmas Tree Cones

Preparation needed: gather resources

Resources: pine cones, modelling clay, milk container tops or bottle tops, glitter, pompoms, sequins, sticks for poking, PVA glue

Age range: early years and lower primary

Group size: any

Additional issues: please use environmentally friendly glitter for this activity. If the pinecones are closed, you may want to bring them inside and place them next to a radiator overnight so that they open to make the 'trees' more effective

Select a pine cone and using clay to secure, stand in the bottle top (stalk end down). Using a small stick, poke pompoms into the crevices then cover in glue to hold in place and decorate with a range of festive sparkles and sequins. You can decorate the bottle top with ribbon or festive tape. If using glitter outside, please use the environmentally friendly version If you want to avoid sparkly bits altogether try tiny balls of scrunched up tissue paper in Christmas colours instead which is very effective.

What are we learning from this activity?
Creating a decoration. Celebrating Christmas, using a range of materials both man made and natural.

Leaf Stencils and Mud Painting

Preparation needed: collect resources

Resources: scissors or you may want to use a craft knife and cutting board, large soft paint brush, pots and water, paper or material to print on. Mud and leaves. Masking tape

Age range: early years, primary, secondary, adult

Group size: small and individual

Additional issues: when using a craft knife ensure that you have a suitable cutting board

Choose some pliable leaves, fresh rather than dry and brittle. Thicker leaves work better with a craft knife, thinner ones with scissors. Cut out shapes from the centre of the leaves. Fix onto paper, card or fabric with masking tape. Mix some mud with a little water. If you are working on material add a little PVA glue so the mud is less likely to flake off when dry. Holding everything steady. Dip the brush into the mud mixture and dab over the leaf stencil in a very gently dabbing motion. Do not brush as this will break the leaf and push the mud under the edges of the stencil. Carefully remove the stencil and allow to dry.

Try over lapping stencils to build up pictures. How about using assorted colours of mud or clays. This also works with squished blackberries. You can also stencil with mud onto trees to leave a trail in the woods for children to follow on a treasure trail.

What are we learning from this activity?
Making our own resources, scissor skills, shapes and using different media to create art work.

Cup Wind Catcher (Robinson anemometer)

Preparation needed: gather resources

Resources: 6 paper cups, wooden skewers, a straw, scissors, clay, strong tape. A card circle or an old CD

Age range: early years, primary, secondary, adult

Group size: work in small groups

Additional issues: simplify for younger children

Meteorologists are people who study the weather. They use an anemometer to measure wind speed. To make a wind catcher take a straw and snip off the bendy bit if it has one. Cut the end of the straw to make 4 flaps and stick to the bottom of one of the cups with strong sticky tape.

Push a wooden skewer through the sides of the cup about half way up to bisect the circle in half. Push a second skewer into the cup at a right angle to the first to make a cross.

Using another skewer make holes half way down 4 cups and attach to the skewers sticking out of the first cup so they are all horizontal to the first cup and all facing the same direction. Press a large lump of clay or playdough onto the CD or card circle. Stick an upturned paper cup into the clay and insert a skewer into the centre of the cup and press down until it is in the clay. Carefully slot the open end of the straw attached to the other cups over the end of the skewer and make sure that the cups can rotate. You may need to trim the straw to size. Mark one of the rotating cups with a large spot. The force of the wind will spin the cups.

Count how many times the spot on the cup passes and you will be able to work out if the wind is stronger or weaker in different areas of your outdoor area. The faster the cups rotate, the faster the wind speed is. Try this experiment on different days and in different areas. Record your results and compare them.

What are we learning from this activity?
The power of the wind, the basics behind wind turbines, counting and comparing, undertaking a scientific experiment.

Olinda's Butterfly Smelly Socks

Preparation needed: gather resources beforehand. You may want the children to help with preparation of scents or use this as a scent matching activity having prepared them in advance

Resources: cotton gloves, mortar and pestle, aroma making materials

Age range: early years and lower primary

Group size: small group

Additional issues: ensure that the children only smell and do not taste

My friend Olinda was looking for activities to demonstrate that butterflies could taste with their feet, so we came up with this one. Prepare a range of aromas using mortar and pestle (alternatively you could use smooth pebbles and flat rocks to grind on).

Ideas for smelly aromas could be crushed orange peel, wild garlic leaves, mashed banana or you could use garlic puree, baking essences such as mint and vanilla or perfume oils.

Mix each aroma separately, add a little water and mix well and pop into a little pot. Ideally 6 different aromas would be nice as butterflies have 6 legs.

You will need to make little butterfly socks. These could be made by cutting off the fingers from cotton gloves, also known as glove liners and are very cheap from chemists and online.

Dip the end of each 'sock' into a different aroma.

Explain to the children that a butterfly was feeling hungry and he wondered what was in each pot but as butterflies have taste receptors on their legs he had dipped his feet to taste what was in each pot. Allow the children to smell each butterfly sock and try to work out where the butterfly had been. Can they match the scents?

This activity would lead nicely into preparing a perfect perfume in the mud kitchen and comparing the different aromas that they could invent by mixing natural ingredients.

What are we learning from this activity?
The location of butterfly olfactory organs, smelling different aromas and matching them to their source.

Mud Painting Bunting

Preparation needed: pre-cut material triangles, gather resources

Resources: pre-cut material triangles, string, pots, mud, sticks, PVA glue, scissors, mortar and pestles if you have them or pebbles and pots, elastic bands

Age range: early years, primary, secondary, adult

Group size: any

Additional issues: make sure hand washing facilities are available

Collect some mud, it may need grinding down to get rid of any lumps, mix with a little water. The addition of some PVA glue will make the mud more flexible and less likely to flake off the material when dry.

You can try making a range of 'paint brushes' by using twigs and natural materials such as leaves, pine needles, feathers, ferns, moss etc, held onto a stick with an elastic band to paint with. Alternatively, finger painting also works well. Decorate some pre-cut material triangles to make effective bunting.

To display the bunting, tie loop some string around a tree or fence post. Double it so you have 2 strings of equal length and twist them together many times to make one string then secure the string to another point. Poke two of the triangles corners into the twists of the string. This is very effective unless it is very windy when you might prefer to use clothes pegs or staples to secure. Use this activity alongside the leaf bashing bunting activity.

What are we learning from this activity?
Experimenting with painting, making own resources, decorating, working as part of a group to make a resource for decoration.

Dandelion Tattoos

Preparation needed: none

Resources: dandelions

Age range: early years, primary, secondary, adult

Group size: any

Additional issues: check for allergies. Ask children not to draw on their faces as parents and schools may not be happy about it. I ask them to limit designs to the back of their hand only

Pick a fresh dandelion including the stalk. Use the white sap from the flower stalk to draw on a tattoo design onto your skin. This will develop over several hours to be light brown and last a couple of days depending on washing activity. Link this activity to tribal markings, runes or mark making. I have used this activity when we were learning about the Stone age and talked about how tribes could identify each other by using symbols. We extended this activity by painting hand marks onto banners using mud to set tribal boundaries.

What are we learning from this activity?
Alternative uses for plants, body art, symbolism and mark making

Stick rafts

Preparation needed: gather resources

Resources: sticks, string, scissors

Age range: early years, primary, secondary, adult

Group size: any

Additional issues: you will need water to test out this activity. Please be aware for water safety and supervise children near water

Gather a range of sticks and lay them side by side. Tie together one at a time, you may want to use 2 or 3 sticks to brace the raft and add strength. You could also build a frame and tie the sticks onto it. Try a range of designs and try them out on some water, either a pond, puddle or stream or a large tray with water in it. Which design floats best? Which one seems more stable? Do different types of sticks work better than others? Is it better to use fresh sticks or dead wood? Can you attach a mast to help the raft sail? Make a sail with a leaf or some paper. Compare with your friends, why not have a race and see which raft can get furthest.

What are we learning from this activity?
Using natural materials, designing and building, experimenting, trial and error. Floating and sinking. Improving designs.

Shadow Theatre

Preparation needed: in order to do this activity, you need a sunny day. String up a tarpaulin between 2 trees with the sun behind it

Resources: tarpaulin, trees, string

Age range: early years, primary, secondary, adult

Group size: any but split into groups and let each group work out their own show to perform to the others

Additional issues: for younger children position an adult either side of the tarpaulin to keep all children in view

String up a tarpaulin (the thin plastic ones seem to work best) or a flat bed sheet (plain rather than patterned works well) between two trees or fixed points so it hangs vertically to make a wall. Ensure that the sun is behind it. Ask the children to make shadows behind the tarpaulin by positioning their bodies close to the plastic sheet. Can the audience guess what they are doing? Try making animal shadows as a group. Can you make an elephant, with one person as the head, two people being flappy ears and someone being a trunk? What other animals can you think of? Using card and scissors you could try making shadow puppets by cutting out shapes and sticking on sticks as handles or making accessories for your human actors such as hats, ears etc and put on a show. Try enacting a simple story like Goldilocks and the Three Bears or The Very Hungry Caterpillar. Perhaps you could progress on to stories and characters from classroom planning, Greek Myths, Saxons or Heroes and Heroines would work well.

I also like to hang up plastic tarpaulins like this in the woods with a supply of mud mixed with water, paintbrushes and rollers for a 'Big Art' painting wall. They are easily hosed down afterwards.

What are we learning from this activity?
Cooperation, working with others, story planning, drama, acting, pretend play, speaking, performing.

Conker Friends

Preparation needed: gather resources

Resources: felt, PVA glue or glue guns, scissors, googly eyes, feathers, pompoms and a conker (the fruit of the horse chestnut tree)

Age range: early years, primary

Group size: any, just make sure there are enough conkers for everybody

Additional issues: check for allergies concerning conkers

The conker is the fruit of the Horse Chestnut Tree and is a large brown smooth shiny seed inside a spiky seed case. Open the seedcase to release the conker.

You may want to combine this activity with going on a conker hunt in autumn (always have a sneaky few spare ones in your pocket just in case anyone is unsuccessful, and you can drop them around for them to find).

Let each child choose a conker. Select some craft materials. Cut out a pair of feet out of felt and stick onto the conker. Decorate to make your conker into a little character.

Why not give your characters names and attribute personalities to them? Why not build them a little house or a mini playground. Try making some conker animals. If you use an awl you can poke holes into the conker shells to poke in twig legs.

What are we learning from this activity?
Making an object using natural and manmade resources. Encouraging animistic play, small person play. Working with others and independently.

Sunflower Den

Preparation needed: this is a spring activity. If you are planting onto grass you may want to remove a ring of turf to make sure that the children plant the seeds in the right place or mark out with string

Resources: sunflower seeds (available from garden centres), an old pencil or dibber, a ruler

Age range: early years, primary, secondary, adult

Group size: small

Additional issues: I have met a child who was allergic to sunflower seeds so please check for allergies prior to doing this activity

Mark out an area you would like to make into a sunflower den (a circle about 1.5 to 2 metres in diameter is good) making sure you leave space for a doorway. Plant sunflower seeds in the ground by making a small hole with a pencil and putting a seed in and covering it. Plant the seeds around the circle about 30 centimetres apart, (for a 2-metre diameter circle you will need approximately 20 seeds). A circle of diameter 3.5 meters should be big enough for a class den!

Water and within a couple of weeks the seeds will have germinated. They will take approximately 2-3 months to reach full height and make great hiding places on school grounds. Why not make lots of circles and make a sunflower village. At the end of the season, the sunflower seeds can be harvested and stored to repeat the activity the following spring, to eat (Please check for food allergies) feed to pets such as rabbits or hamsters or to feed to wild birds in the winter. Birds like pecking the seeds from the flower heads or you could remove and put on a bird table.

Alternatively, seeds can be planted in small pots or egg trays and observed in the classroom until germinated then transferred outside when established.

What are we learning from this activity?

Planning, circles, diameters, circumferences, planting, growing, harvesting seeds. Growing plants, growing crops, germinating seeds.

Leaf Identifying Bunting

Preparation needed: collect resources, prepare bunting, display

Resources: a range of leaves from your outdoor area, card, pen, scissors, ID Charts or books, laminator, laminating sheets, hole punch, string

Age range: early years, primary, secondary, adult

Group size: any

Additional issues: please be aware that laminators can become hot when using, remove thick stalks

This reusable resource will be helpful for children and participants to identify leaves from your outdoor area. Collect a range of leaves from trees, bushes or plants from your outdoor area. Identify the leaves and write a label for each one. Laminate the leaves including the label. Trim to make triangle shaped bunting or leave as rectangles if you prefer. Hole punch the top of the bunting with a couple of holes and thread through string. Display by stringing the bunting between trees or along a fence. When in your outdoor area encourage children to try and match leaves that they find with the laminated key. This is a good start to using means of identification for children, it is also specific to your area. Ask children to search the area and find leaves which match those on the bunting. If you have plants that are poisonous you could identify that on the bunting, so the children know which ones not to touch.

What are we learning from this activity?
Matching, using resources to identify, developing investigation skills.

Reindeer Bell Sticks

Preparation needed: gather resources

Resources: sticks, googly eyes, red mini pompoms, PVA glue, wool, bells

Age range: early years, primary

Group size: any

Additional issues: if the deer are going to be used in a concert or have rough treatment you may want to use a glue gun for a more durable finish

This is a lovely, simple Christmas activity perfect to use as a visual prop and accessory for a Christmas concert when singing 'Rudolph the Red Nosed Reindeer' for Early Years children.

Find some twigs with a Y shaped fork in them. Tie a strand or even 2 strands of contrasting wool to the bottom of the Y and wind the wool around the lower part of the stick working your way up the stick. Just before you get to the fork tie on a small bell or two onto the stick. (you can find these in craft shops) Tie tightly to fix. Glue some googly eyes and a mini pompom nose in the fork of the stick. When it is dry you can hold onto the wool 'handle' and shake your reindeer bells. These make lovely take home presents.

What are we learning from this activity?
Music, making props and musical accompaniment, winding, tying, gluing, selecting and using natural and manmade resources, group singing and rhythm.

Pet Logs

Preparation needed: scatter logs around your area for the children to find

Resources: small logs, felt tips or marker pens, rope or paracord

Age range: early years and lower primary

Group size: any but make sure there are enough logs for everyone to have one

Additional issues: if children run with the log there is the chance it can bounce and catch their ankles so please make them aware of this

This is one of the cutest activities I have done and encourages loads of child led play afterwards. Ask the children to find themselves a log that they like the look of. Make sure that there are a range of small logs available ideally no longer than a forearm from wrist to elbow and about the diameter or maybe a little bigger than the fore arm. Let the children decorate their log by drawing a face on one end with marker pens or even charcoal although this does not tend to remain on the log for long if the ground is damp or they are handled and cuddled a lot. They then need to give their log a name. Show the children how to tie knots so that they can 'tie a lead' onto their log, elephant knots, clove hitches and the good old reef knots work well.

Take your pet log for a walk, build him a home, play with him, let him visit other pet logs in the area.

What are we learning from this activity?
Using body measurements, choosing natural resources, decorating, pretend play, animistic play, nurturing, thinking about the needs of others.

Christmas Tree Print Cards

Preparation needed: gather resources

Resources: ferns or bracken, green paint, paper, sequins, pva glue, paint roller

Age range: early years, primary, secondary, adult

Group size: any

Additional issues: some ferns and bracken can be toxic if eaten. Please ensure children wash their hands after handling. Also, do not pull at a bracken plant stem but pick the fronds or use scissors as they can cause paper cut type abrasions on hands if you do

Using a paint roller apply green paint to a fern or bracken. Place paint down onto a sheet of paper or card. Place another sheet on top and gently press down and smooth with a hand or a clean paint roller.

Remove the top sheet of paper then carefully peel off the fern. A print on the fern will be left on the paper. Leave to dry. Cut out and use to decorate Christmas cards. Decorate with sequins and glitter for a festive feel. If completing the decorating outside, please use environmentally friendly glitter.

What are we learning from this activity?
Making items using natural resources, using paint, using rollers, printing, sticking.

Stick and String Christmas Tree

Preparation needed: gather resources

Resources: string, scissors, beads, ribbon straight sticks of varying lengths

Age range: early years, primary, secondary, adult

Group size: any

Additional issues: children may need help lashing on the horizontal sticks

Choose a range of sticks in graduating lengths. Arrange into a triangle shape. Select a long straight stick to be the trunk and lash on the first stick at the centre point at right angles about a third of the way up the stick, lash on the second stick and graduate the length of the sticks as you work your way up the 'trunk' stick to form a triangle shape. Decorate with ribbon and beads. If you are taking them home, you may want to stick on some sequins and glitter.

Display by either pushing the trunk stick into the ground or a plant pot. Alternatively, you may want to hang it.

Please see the tool section for making Stick and wire Christmas trees as an alternative.

What are we learning from this activity?
Making an object, celebration of festivals, estimating and ordering, graduating sizes tying knots, decorating.

Rain Painting

Preparation needed: check the weather forecast, gather resources

Resources: a rainy day, paper, food colourings, paints or powder paints, pebbles or stones

Age range: early years, primary

Group size: any

Additional issues: if ground is already wet it may be good to lay the paper on a plastic sheet, tray or tarpaulin

Lay paper on the ground, use pebbles or stones to weigh the corners of the paper down. Splodge some paint or food colouring onto the paper and let the rain do the work. The rain water will spread and mix the colours. Try this activity with powder paint by sprinkling dry powder paint onto the paper and watch as the paint dissolves in the rain drops. When you are happy with the result, move the finished painting to a dry area and leave to dry. If you hang the paper up vertically, you can get some interesting dribble effects.

If you would like to make a large group painting using a roll of wall lining paper works well.

What are we learning from this activity?
Weather, rain, colours, making art, selecting and using colours, working with others.

Sponge Ball

Preparation needed: gather resources. For young children you may want to make these in advance

Resources: sponges (assorted colours) dental floss, sharp scissors

Age range: early years, primary, secondary, adult

Group size: any

Additional issues: use the flat type of sponges used for cleaning or in the kitchen

Cut the sponges into strips about the width of an adult finger. Gather together 12 'fingers' and twist slightly in the middle and tie tightly with string or dental floss in the middle to secure.

Use your sponge balls to practice throwing and catching. Great for little ones as they are light, soft, very visible and not smooth so less likely to slip from little fingers. These are a fantastic addition to water play activities. You can also use them for painting activities or as an additional resource to use for teabag painting. How about for older children on a sweltering day supplying each team with a water bucket and lots of sponge balls each and have a soggy sponge ball battle. This can give and extra dimension to games like stalking or capture the flag. This is also good for the group painting challenge as they hold lots of paint! (Easily rinsed out and you can pop them in the washing machine to use again on another day).

What are we learning from this activity?
Throwing and catching, water play, team games, art work, painting, creating resources, colours, properties of sponge.

Fluffy Owlets

Preparation needed: gather resources, make sure the pinecones have been warm and dry so that they are open

Resources: pine cones, cotton wool, a pokey stick, PVA glue, googly eyes, feathers for wings

Age range: early years, primary, secondary, adult

Group size: any but ensure there are enough pinecones for everybody

Additional issues: none

Owls are nocturnal birds with large eyes and flat faces, they can turn their heads up to 270 degrees and fly almost silently to swoop and catch their prey using their talons (claws). They hunt small mammals, insects, birds and some species even catch fish. They regurgitate indigestible bits of their prey like fur, bones and feathers in owl pellets. If you are lucky enough to find an owl pellet, soak it in warm water for an hour and then ease it apart to discover what the owls has been eating. There are around 200 different species of owl with 5 main species living in the UK which are the Tawny owl with its twit twoo call, the Barn owl with its heart shaped face and white underside, the Little owl, the short-eared owl, the long-eared owl and there are also visiting species of owl like the snowy owl and the European Eagle owl. Most owls are solitary or paired birds but if you were to get a group of owls, it is called a parliament!

Owls do not build their nests but tend to use holes they find or use squirrel dreys. Many owls like using nest boxes. Owls lay white eggs and the mother owl incubates the egg while the father bird hunts to provide the food. When the owlets are larger and can maintain their own body temperature, the mother also hunts for food. When owls are little they are fluffy with big eyes.

Find an open pinecone. Secure the stalk end of your pinecone on a small piece of clay to balance it upside down. Dab glue into the open leaves of the pinecone. Using a small stick, poke cotton wool into every gap. Stick on some googly eyes, either the type you can get in a craft shop or stickers and a beak made of card to complete the owlet. Making a home for your owlet in a hollow of a tree? Maybe share a story such as Owl Babies by Martin Waddell.

What are we learning from this activity?
All about owls, habitats, using natural resources, fine motor skills.

Teabag Painting

Preparation needed: gather resources, a sunny day

Resources: a selection of different flavoured tea bags both the fruit sort and the usual variety, boiling water, small pots or a paint pallet tray, brushes, paper or card, straws

Age range: early years, although a group of adults loved this activity too

Group size: small groups

Additional issues: using those out of date fruit tea bags in the back of the cupboard is fine for this activity

This is a lovely olfactory and visual activity.

Pour a little hot water into each pot and put a different tea bag in each one. Let the water cool down. Using the paintbrushes or the teabags themselves splodge the coloured water onto the paper, tilt the paper to let the liquid drip, using the straws blow the liquid to make interesting shapes and add assorted colours to make lovely art work with beautiful aromas. This works well with watercolour paper. I have also done this activity with children who were partially sighted. To make the colours more visible when dried I added some food colourings and they painted with aromas.

What are we learning from this activity?
Using items for different uses than their intended use, smells and aromas, creating a piece of art, colours.

Fairy doors

Preparation needed: gather resources

Resources: twigs or lolly pop sticks, glue, string, natural materials to decorate

Age range: early years, primary

Group size: any

Additional issues: also make fairy ladders to make your outdoor area even more enchanted

Collect together a range of small straight sticks of similar length (alternatively you can use lolly pop sticks) and fashion a small door. You can use string or glue to fix them together. Find natural materials to decorate your door and find a suitable hollow in the base of a tree to rest your door against. You may want to decorate the area by making a small garden path and garden. Try making a small window to complement your door and add more doors to other trees to make your outdoor area into fairyland. Small ladders made with string and twigs and hung in trees also encourage children's imaginative play. Use along with stick fairies to encourage children in their small person, imaginative and animistic play.

What are we learning from this activity?
Making play resources, collecting, selecting, using natural materials, design, tying, sticking, decorating, imaginative play.

Tic Tac Toe Stones

Preparation needed: gather resources

Resources: 10 pebbles, chalk or felt tip pens, 4 long straight sticks

Age range: early years, primary

Group size: pairs

Additional issues: none

Lay out a grid with the sticks of 2 parallel sticks crossed at right angles with two more parallel sticks in a hashtag formation #. Make sure that the squares formed by the sticks are big enough to place pebbles in. Each player takes 5 pebbles each and decorates the pebbles the same, for instance one person may have their pebbles decorated with ladybirds and the other person with bumblebees. Each person takes it in turns to place one of their pebbles in the grid. The idea of the game is to achieve three pebbles the same in a straight row either vertically, horizontally or diagonally on the grid. You can encourage children to make this activity more challenging by adding in more sticks and stones so 6 sticks and 16 stones or 8 sticks and 26 stones. How about making the challenge that you must get 4 in a row?

What are we learning from this activity?
Making our own games, adding a new twist to traditional games, painting, turn taking, problem solving, planning, extending activities, making up new rules.

Skeletons

Preparation needed: print out some pictures of animal skeletons

Resources: pictures of skeletons, natural materials

Age range: primary, secondary, adult

Group size: any but split into smaller groups

Additional issues: none

Talk to the children about skeletons and how they differ for diverse types of animals. This is a good opportunity to explore mammals, reptiles and birds. You may want to look at human skeletons as well. Show the children pictures of different animal and bird skeletons and see if they can guess which animal they belong to.

Look around for natural objects and replicate the skeleton using twigs, leaves, stones etc. Can other people guess what animal the skeleton belongs to? If you have any animal skeletons this would be a great resource to complement this activity

This activity links well with the book Funny Bones, projects of about me, classification of living things and biology.

What are we learning from this activity?
Skeletal structures of different types of animals, using natural resources.

Shadow Water Painting

Preparation needed: gather resources, this activity needs to be done on a sunny day

Resources: bucket of water, large (decorator type) paint brushes, playground or paving

Age range: early years, primary, secondary, adult

Group size: 3 or 4 in a group

Additional issues: you need to work quickly if it is a very hot day

On a sunny day find an area that people can cast shadows on the ground. Experiment making different poses until they find the one they like best. Get one child to make a shape with their body and the other children need to 'paint' their shadow with water. Use large paint brushes or empty washing up liquid bottles for a quick result. As this is a very temporary art work, it is a great idea to capture the results on camera. This also works well for objects such as tools, trees, twigs or toys.

What are we learning from this activity?
Using our bodies to make shapes, holding a pose, staying still, following an outline, using a different resource, properties of water, evaporation, splashing, spreading, exploring shadows.

Shadow Paper Tracing

Preparation needed: gather resources, this activity needs to be done on a sunny day

Resources: White paper (wall lining paper works well), charcoal or mud

Age range: early years, primary, secondary, adult

Group size: small groups work well but you can have many groups working at one time

Additional issues: have hand washing facilities as this is quite a mucky activity. This works well as an activity used in conjunction with shadow theatre and shadow water painting

On a sunny day find a position where you can cast a shadow with your body. Lay the paper on the ground and trace around the outline with charcoal or mud. Fill in the shape with natural objects such as leaves and twigs. If you want this to be a more permanent piece of work, use glue to stick on the leaves etc, Decorate the body shape Aboriginal style by using mud and clays with finger and stick painting. You can also try capturing the shadow of objects such as leaves and sticks.

This activity also works if a person lies on the ground and the rest of the team outlines the body shape with twigs before the person gets up carefully. Then the body shape can be filled in with natural objects.

What are we learning from this activity?
Working as a team, staying still, shadows, shade, sunshine, using mud or charcoal as an art medium.

Shell Fairy Houses

Preparation needed: none

Resources: a beach with shells, permanent felt tip pens (Sharpies)

Age range: early years, primary, secondary, adult

Group size: any

Additional issues: none except permanent pens do not come off skin so be careful

Instigate a beach hunt and search for a variety of empty shells. Limpet shells work very well. Brush any sand off the shells and make sure that they are dry. Draw little houses on the shells using permanent marker pens, windows, doors etc and arrange your shells into a fairy village. Decorate the village with seaweed gardens, pebble paths and drift wood and seaweed trees. You can make little winkle Cars to drive along the pebble roads. Make any interesting beach finds to be centre pieces of the village and play beach fairies. This is a lovely activity to instigate imaginative play with miniature worlds and cooperation with others to build a sizable village. These make a great addition to a sand pit or an outdoor area and often children will revisit them again and again.

If you do not want to use this resource again you can use normal felt tip pens which will wash off in warm soapy water when you have finished the activity but please be aware the pen will smudge onto children's fingers more easily.

What are we learning from this activity?
Finding and making our own resources using natural materials.

Leaf Collection

Preparation needed: this activity works very well on an Autumn day as the leaves tend to be a bit more pliable and less crumbly. Collect resources

Resources: pipe cleaners, large beads and lots of fallen autumn leaves

Age range: early years, early primary

Group size: any

Additional issues: none

Prepare a pipe cleaner for assembling a leaf collection by threading a large bead onto the end and folding over the end to stop it coming off. (Elder beads work great for this – see later in the book for instructions.)

Thread leaves onto the pipe cleaner by making a hole in the centre of a leaf and gently pushing it onto the end of the pipe cleaner. Wiggle it gently and push it down to where the bead is stopping the leaves from falling off the end. Select another leaf and repeat the process. Make a collection of colourful autumn leaves. This is a great travelling activity which complements autumnal walks. It is also a wonderful way to collect leaves of all different shapes, sizes and colours to sort and compare later in the classroom if you carefully remove them from the pipe cleaner when you return. Alternatively, if you loop the top over a completed wire you can hang it up as a decoration to display the colours of autumn.

What are we learning from this activity?
Fine motor skills, personal artwork using natural resources, choosing and selecting resources, colours, shades and spectrums, making an item and threading, signs of Autumn.

Magnet Dangling

Preparation needed: gather resources

Resources: small hoop magnets, sticks, string, paper clips, string, marker pens, paper and pencils to keep score

Age range: early years, primary, secondary, adult

Group size: any

Additional issues: the shorter the string, the easier it is to control the fishing rod to 'catch' a leaf fish. If a child is struggling to catch anything, shorten their string

Collect a range of leaves of different shapes and colours and pop a paper clip on each one. Make a string circle on the ground and put the leaves into it. Ask the children to find a stick about the length of their forearm and tie on a piece of string (the length of your arm span) Tie a magnet on to the other end of the string and dangle the magnet into the string circle and see which leaf you can catch.

This game can be used for a range of activities:

LEAF ADDITION: write numbers on the leaves, add together your catch, the highest score wins.

LEAF WORDS: write sounds or letters on the leaves and fish to make words, for example have a leaf with 'IP' on it laid by the side of the pond. The children fish for letter leaves, have letters and sounds like H, L, R, D, K, N, S, T, P, Z and 'SH', CH, BL, DR etc.

FORFEITS: write challenges on the leaves, for example 'sing a song', 'Tell a joke', 'do a dance'.

CHARADES: write a charade to be performed on each leaf, maybe to mime an animal for others to guess.

What are we learning from this activity?
Using body measurements, collecting resources, using natural resources, magnets, fine motor and gross motor skills, patience, perseverance, turn taking, sound blends, addition, mathematics.

Pebble Tracks

Preparation needed: none if you have smooth pebbles in your area but if not, you can buy pebbles from DIY stores and garden centres

Resources: pebbles, chalks or permanent felt tip pens (Sharpies)

Age range: early years, primary

Group size: any

Additional issues: none except permanent pens do not come off skin so be careful

Collect a range of smooth pebbles (either from your area or buy in a garden centre or builders merchants.) Draw lines on the pebbles using Permanent pens if you want this to last as a resource or with chalks if you want it to be a temporary activity. Starting at one edge of the pebble and finishing on a different side. Include squiggles, wavy lines curves and straight lines. Give this to the children as an open-ended resource and see how they play with them. Many children will join up the lines on one pebble to match the lines on other pebbles to make a continuous track whereas others will sort the pebbles according to the type of lines drawn on them. If you want to extend this play you can also use multiple colours and draw half the line with one colour and finish the line with another colour. The children can then use these as colour matching dominos to make a continuous track. I also keep in my bag a pack of tiny cars, people and animals when playing with younger children (the type you may use in the classroom for counting and grouping) and this can extend the children's play further.

What are we learning from this activity?
Matching, lining up, sorting, working creatively and working cooperatively with others

4

Using Tools with children

Using tools when outside with children can add a whole new dimension to their learning. As well as learning a new range of safety skills which will ultimately promote their independence and risk management skills, using tools can make the whole learning experience more diverse. Children will be using tasks to enable them to complete specific tasks. They will discover that using the right equipment for the right job can save them a lot of time and effort and is something that is transferable to the skills they will need as an adult in the workaday world. Using tools will also promote their strength, stamina, dexterity and coordination skills as well as helping them to achieve tasks and succeed, building their self-esteem and feelings of self-worth.

Tools must be sharp and in good condition to be safe, a blunt knife is more likely to cause frustration and accidents than a sharp one, a saw

Safety when outdoors is paramount. Although it is not desirable to wrap children up in cotton wool and remove all risk from every activity, tools are sharp and can harm our charges so following safety rules and procedures and enforcing them at all times is very important. It is also important that the task set is appropriate, safe and achievable for the level, skill base and ability of the child.

Before you start using tools with children become confident in your own abilities to use each tool in a safe and correct manner. You need to practice to become a competent user. There are various courses and mentoring which may help you increase your confidence and competence when using tools, for instance TCV who are a group of conservation volunteers and The National Trust are often happy to support your tool learning skills in exchange for some volunteering hours. It is also worth getting in touch with your local wildlife trust as they run volunteer weekends.

The child needs to be supported when using any tool and I would suggest that there is a ratio of one adult to one child initially until the child is a competent user, and even then, ensure that the child is always observable and in a delegated area to keep other people using the area safe. In many situations a rope safety circle will suffice.

The Rope Safety Circle

I introduce a rope safety circle during outdoor sessions so that children have a visual barrier to demarcate areas they must not enter unless invited. Children learn before the introduction of tools or fire, the importance of the 'safety circle'

We learn that if the circle is on the ground we always walk around it and never through it. This is achieved through reinforcement by playing circle games that ensure that no one enters the circle.

I have used this method for many years and with practice children, even as young as 2 are able to recognise that the safety circle is not to be entered unless the child is invited by the adult.

When using the rope circle go to the edge of the circle and invite the child to accompany you to the centre to use the tools or approach the fire. When the child has finished accompany them back to the edge of the circle and invite the next one to join you. If you have lots of adults assisting you may want more than one adult in the circle using tools with children, if this is the case ensure that the circle is large enough for you all to work comfortably and do not allow children to stray into other tool use zones whilst in the circle.

Always remember that children need to be confident and comfortable outside with themselves, the people they are with and the environment they are in before they will become comfortable and confident using tools.

There are a range of tools that are used outside with children

A tool is seen as an object which will help you achieve a job. Starting with the most basic tools that we may use with children outside.

PPE

Personal Protective Equipment is often referred to as PPE and consists of equipment that will keep an individual safe, for instance a safety helmet, goggles, heavy duty gloves, clothing and footwear to protect from the weather and the environment. In the context of outdoor learning with children, the most commonly utilised PPE is in the form of clothing.

When taking children outside it is a good idea to dress for the environment and weather. In chilly weather this should consist of a warm base layer, warm layered clothing, waterproof and windproof jacket and trousers, wellington boots or sturdy outdoor boots, hats and gloves. In hot weather make sure that the child is suitably dressed. I recommend wearing long sleeves and trousers to protect exposed skin from scratches, insect bites and sunburn as well as a brimmed hat. Make sure that exposed skin has sun cream applied.

Scissors

What is this tool? Two blades with finger holes at one end, joined by a swivel pin that allow the cutting edges to be opened and closed.

What will we use it for? Used to cut paper, string, card, material, leaves, stems.

How do we safely use it? Taking my Grannies advice, never run with scissors! Hold the closed blades in the palm of your hand when walking with scissors or passing them to someone else. Hold the object you are cutting with one hand and made sure to keep your fingers out of the way when snipping. Use the correct scissors for the job, for instance children's scissors suitable for cutting paper and leaves will struggle to cut through material or thick card.

You may want to have a selection of left and right-handed scissors. For younger or less able children there are dual handled training scissors for an adult and child to use simultaneously.

How do we care for this tool? Ensure that the scissors are clean. Take some sand paper with the sandy side facing down a cut 3 or 4 strips which will sharpen the blades. This can also be done using aluminium foil. Fold it several times and cut into strips with the scissors. You can also sharpen using a whetstone (see below).

Ideas of activities that we can do using this tool: cutting holes and shapes in leaves for mud stencil painting, cutting string for a wide variety of activities, snipping of leaf stems to make leaf crowns, cutting material for forest friend clothing.

Mallets

What is this tool? A mallet is a type of hammer with a large head, usually made of wood or rubber. Mallets are one of the earliest tools used that we know about. Evidence of mallets being buried as grave goods have been found in stone age graves.

What will we use it for? To knock together pieces of wood or drive cutting tools like billhooks and chisels. May also be used to flatten objects.

How do we safely use it? Make sure you keep fingers out of the way of the mallet. If using a mallet with another person, for instance making a wooden mallet, make sure that you both make eye contact before a blow is struck.

How do we care for this tool? Wipe clean with a damp cloth, check the head for damage, replace the head when worn.

Ideas of activities that we can do using this tool: mallet making, hapa zome (leaf bashing), knocking sticks into the ground, tent pegs, directing a chisel when wood carving.

Knives

What is this tool? A knife is a tool which consists of a thin, sharp edged metal blade and a handle and is used for cutting. When using knives with children it is important to emphasise that knives are tools for doing a job like cutting bread, chopping vegetables or in this instance for whittling wood. Do not refer to them as weapons.

What will we use it for? Cutting, chopping, whittling, splitting sticks etc.

How do we safely use it? Knives should always be stored in a safe container, preferably stored within a tool bag or tool box. Never wear a glove on the hand that is holding the knife. You can wear a safety glove on the non-tool hand however things can sometimes slip in a gloved hand. Always cut away from yourself, never towards yourself. Do not sit and work on your knees, work to one side or preferably stand in one spot. If you need to sit (for instance because of mobility problems, do so astride a log or with a rubber mat laid over the legs (the type you put in a car). Do not walk around when using a knife.

When using a knife with children I always advocate the adult standing behind the child with their hands guiding the child's movements until the child can achieve the correct motion and angle to work effectively. By standing behind the child, the adult is there to help and guide without being in the child's line of vision and without being in front of the blade.

How do we care for this tool? Check knives before use, a blunt knife can lead to frustration and cause accidents. Keep knives sharp to be effective. Sharpen using a whet stone.

Ideas of activities that we can do using this tool: whittling the end of sticks for marshmallow toasting, whittling the end of a stick to make a forest friend, removing wood to make a kazoo, shaping the handle on a wooden mallet, making feather sticks to decorate or use as kindling for the fire, removing small sections of bark to make patterns on a walking stick, making a wooden spatula or spoon (a specialist knife called a crook knife will enable you to shape the bowl of a spoon).

Loppers

What is this tool? Loppers are a type of scissors or secateurs with long handles. There are several types of loppers that we may use

- Bypass loppers, where blade and bill slide past each other like scissors and are good for close, clean cuts on live branches up to about 3.5 cms in diameter. Dead wood tends to get stuck in the blades.
- Anvil loppers, where a blade chops against the anvil plate. Not to be used on live wood as the anvil crushes soft stems and you do not achieve a clean cut. Anvil loppers are suitable for using on dead wood up to 5 cm diameter.

What will we use it for? Cutting sticks of various thicknesses to the required length

How do we safely use it? When using loppers or saws to do heavy work it is advisable to wear steel toe capped boots to protect yourself, a hard hat if you are working overhead. Hold at arm's length and position the loppers where you want to cut and draw the handles together. If you find that you lack arm strength, ratchet loppers are available which allow you to cut through a branch gradually without removing the blades. Try to make sure that there is a clean cut, slightly angled if you are cutting from a live tree so water will drain from it rather than sitting on the open cut.

When using loppers with children I demonstrate by cutting a thick stick with the loppers and passing it round the group. I ask them to look at the diameter of their finger in comparison to the diameter of the stick (the stick is always bigger) We talk about the safety involved and emphasis.

How do we care for this tool? Check the tool for damage, clean the blades them wipe with an oiled cloth. Sharpen blades using a whetstone. Store in a secure, dry place.

Ideas of activities that we can do using this tool: cutting sticks to make forest friends, picture frames, kazoos, whistles, magic wands, walking sticks, looms, bows and arrows, etc.

Secateurs

What is this tool? Secateurs are scissor like tools much smaller than loppers and are also known as pruning shears or hand pruners and used by holding in one hand.

Like loppers above, there are two main types of secateurs, bypass and anvil.

What will we use it for? Snipping twigs and pruning shoots

How do we safely use it? Left handed secateurs are available. Make sure that the secateurs are not too big for your hands or for use by children. Demonstrate that they have sharp blades and can cut through shoots the same size as a small child's fingers. Children must keep both hands on the secateurs handles at all times. It they use them one handed there is a greater risk of them catching fingers. For older children with bigger hands if their spare hand wanders close to the blade, I ask them to hold the secateurs with one hand and hold the wrist of the tool hand with the other hand.

How do we care for this tool? Check the tool for damage, clean the blades them wipe with an oiled cloth. Sharpen blades using a whetstone. Store in a secure, dry place.

Ideas of activities that we can do using this tool: snipping twigs for various uses, cutting willow whips to make stars, hearts, wands, dream catcher etc. Cutting twigs to make charcoal in a tin.

Billhooks

What is this tool? A Billhook is a tool used for cutting woody plants such as small branches and saplings in hedge laying and coppicing and for removing twigs and side-shoots from a branch. (This is known as removing the brash or snedding) It is a cross between a knife and axe usually made with medium carbon steel with a long straight blade of 20-25 cms long which curves towards the end. Billhooks usually have a tang which passes through its wooden handle which is often made of ash as this strong and can stand repeated impact. Some billhooks known as double edged billhooks have a blade along their back. This variety are not suitable for using with children.

What will we use it for? For removing brash from branches and splitting wood.

How do we safely use it? When removing brash from a branch, always use with the blade going away from the body in a sweeping motion. Do not use gloves on your tool hand. Wear safety boots and a hard hat if coppicing or working with poles, spars or branches above head height. Never leave a billhook on the ground. Return it to the tool bag or embed it in a log.

How do we care for this tool? Wipe the tool with a damp cloth to remove any dirt and debris. Check the handle and blade. Sharpen the blade only on the inside of the curve with a whetstone. When the blade is sharpened wipe with an oily cloth. Always carry a billhook in a tool bag.

Ideas of activities that we can do using this tool: den building, making kazoos, mallet making, making kindling.

Bow saws

What is this tool? A bow saw is a frame saw with the frame making a rainbow shaped bow. It has a coarse wide blade with many teeth which is held in tension by the frame.

What will we use it for? Cutting wood and branches up to about 6 inches in diameter.

How do we safely use it? Make sure that the wood is securely held so it will not bounce or move when you are sawing. A low fork in a tree works well. Keep your non-tool hand away from the blade at all times. When using a bowsaw with children I ask them to keep both hands on the bowsaw handle. If cutting a small log, for instance to make tree cookies I pre-cut a small groove for each tree cookie to be cut and the children then have a starting point. With older children I ask that they put their hand through the bow to hold the wood while they start a saw cut and keep their hand in position until the blade is embedded in the wood. Move the holding hand back through the bow and hold the branch about a body width distance from the blade. Make sure that the saw cut is opening rather than compressing when you are cutting, adjust the position of the wood accordingly. If you need intricate cutting, use a hacksaw (small version of a bowsaw with an added handle and a fine blade). Do not wear a glove on the tool hand. Make sure that when not being used, the cover is replaced on the blade and hang it up out of reach or replace in tool bag rather than leaving it lying on the ground.

How do we care for this tool? Check your bowsaw for signs of wear and defects. Carefully wipe any debris from the blade. Cover with a blade cover when not in use, even when in a bag. If the bowsaw is being stored for a while, wipe the blade with an oiled cloth. The blade is easy to replace when needed. When you change the blade of a bowsaw, use it a few times yourself to wear the blade in before allowing children to use it.

Ideas of activities that we can do using this tool: Cutting poles for den building, making tree cookies, cutting wood and branches to size for using for a range of projects.

Folding or retracting saws

What is this tool? A folding or retracting saw is a blade that folds or retracts into the handle of the saw.

What will we use it for? This is a useful tool for cutting small branches and poles especially ones that are too big for loppers but difficult for a bowsaw to reach.

How do we safely use it? Fold out or pull out the blade. Make sure that it is firmly secured and will not fold back in on itself or slip into the handle. Make sure that the handle is comfortable to hold and not too big for your hand. When working with a small child I embed the blade within the wood by making a few saw strokes then ask them to hold the handle with both hands and pull back and forth. For non-confident children they put a hand on top of my hand whilst I am using the saw, so they feel the vibration and feel the movement of the saw. When using the saw, make sure that the hand holding the wood is well out of the way for the blade.

How do we care for this tool? Regularly check the blade is in good condition and replace when necessary. With a new blade, wear in a few times before allowing children and young people to use it. Check the folding or sliding mechanism is secure.

Ideas of activities that we can do using this tool: Cutting poles for den building, cutting wood and small branches to size for using for a range of projects.

Hacksaws

What is this tool? A hacksaw is a fine-toothed saw with a D shaped frame which holds a blade under tension.

What will we use it for? Hacksaws, although often used to cut metal, can be used to cut small pieces of wood. Hacksaws are often seen in Nursery settings in the wood work corner and are often children's first experience of using tools independently. A hack saw is also small and more manageable making it easier to access awkward areas.

How do we safely use it? Always keep holding hand away from the blade. Firmly grip the handle and draw forward and backwards to embed the blade in the wood. Keep a nice steady rhythm going to cut through the wood.

How do we care for this tool? Check the frame and blade before use and change the blade when necessary.

Ideas of activities that we can do using this tool: Making small objects such as a model raft, a miniature catapult, puppets etc.

Hand Drills

What is this tool? A manually operated drill which amplifies the circular movement of the turning crank to turn the bit and drill a hole. Usually used for woodworking.

What will we use it for? A hand drill is useful for drilling a range of size of holes, holding drill bits from 1mm to 9mm.

How do we safely use it? Clamp the wood you are drilling or ask someone else to hold it securely for you. Hold the drill vertically and turn in a clockwise direction. I often find that 2 children can use this tool very efficiently together.

How do we care for this tool? Regularly check the working mechanisms of this tool. lubricate with a spot of oil if it is stiff or squeaky. Check the drill bits are straight and replace if necessary.

Ideas of activities that we can do using this tool: Anything that requires drilled holes in wood, tree cookies, puppets, twig trees, beads.

Palm Drills

What is this tool? A palm drill is a drill bit mounted secured into a handle, small and light.

What will we use it for? Drilling holes, especially useful for children and where charging batteries or portability is important. It is a useful tool when drilling a small number of holes or if you need lots of drills for a group to use at the same time as palm drills are relatively cheap to buy and light to carry.

How do we safely use it? We use a palm drill safely by positioning the wood to be drilled either on the ground or firm surface. Do not drill into your hand or leg. Press down and twist.

How do we care for this tool? Check on a regular basis for wear on the handle a drill bit. Replace as necessary. It is possible to make your own palm drill by fixing a drill bit into a wooden handle or alternatively make your own handle by using hand mouldable plastic (also known as polymorph). I have used this to make customised handles for children who need adaptable tools.

Ideas of activities that we can do using this tool: Tree cookie medals, inserting dowling axels into cookie wheels to make vehicles, puppets.

Awl

What is this tool? A sharp point on a wooden handle.

What will we use it for? Making a starting hole for either drilling a hole, inserting a screw or guiding a nail. May be used to scratch markings into wood or even make holes in leather and material.

How do we safely use it? Set wood or material onto a firm surface, position awl and hold securely as you apply pressure to make the required hole or mark.

How do we care for this tool? Check for wear, sharpen point on whet stone as required.

Ideas of activities that we can do using this tool: Making holes or starting holes to prepare for drilling, bug hotels, tree cookie activities.

Brace and bit

What is this tool? This is a robust type of hand drill and holds larger drill bits than a traditional hand drill.

What will we use it for? Drilling larger holes in wood.

How do we safely use it? Hold the drill vertically and turn in a clockwise direction.

How do we care for this tool? Check the drill bits regularly and replace as necessary. Intermittently rub an oily cloth over the metal parts to prevent rusting.

Ideas of activities that we can do using this tool: Anything that requires drilled holes in wood, tree cookies, puppets, twig trees, beads, doweling axels into cookie wheels to make vehicles.

Electric drills

What is this tool? A battery or mains operated drill.

What will we use it for? Drilling holes in wood.

How do we safely use it? Fix in drill bit and secure. Mark a guide hole to stop the bit slipping. Select speed and direction. Position drill making sure that the wood to be drilled is held securely. and gently press whilst pressing the 'on' button. To remove drill bit from wood, change the switch to reverse mode.

How do we care for this tool? Check regularly, charge before use, store in box provided.

Ideas of activities that we can do using this tool: anything that requires drilled holes in wood, tree cookies, puppets, twig trees, beads.

5

Activities using tools

Bubble Wands

Preparation needed: collect resources and equipment. You may want to pre-cut elder sticks and wires

Resources: wire, wire cutters, chunky beads, elder sticks, loppers, tent pegs, bubble mixture

Age range: early years, primary, secondary, adult

Group size: any but younger children will need assistance

Additional issues: caution is needed when using loppers and wire cutters. Make sure all wire ends are tucked inside the handle to prevent scratches, beware of bubble mixture getting near eyes

Cut elder sticks 10-20 cms long. Using a tent peg push out the pith in the centre of the stick. This will form the bubble wand handle. Cut a piece of wire 3 times the length of the handle. fashion a loop in the centre of the wire and twist the wire to secure. Thread on some beads, (wooden ones look particularly nice but any chunky beads which are bigger than the elder pith hole will do) Thread the wires through the elder handle and add another bead at the base of the wand. Wrap the wire around the bead and push back through so the ends of the wire are secured within the elder handle.

You can bind the handle with coloured thread for added decoration.

These wands make lovely gifts for children to take home and work well when combined with magical or fantasy activities

What are we learning from this activity?
Designing and making a resource, Design technology, threading, cutting, pushing, using natural and manmade materials, blowing bubbles

Easy Bubble Mixture

Preparation needed: collect resources

Resources: 1 litre hot water 250 mls quality washing up liquid, 4 table spoons of glycerine

Age range: early years, primary, secondary, adult

Group size: small group

Additional issues: care is needed when using hot water

Mix together a litre of hot water gently with 250 mls of quality washing up liquid (cheap, very runny washing up liquid does not work very well at all. Stir in 4 table spoons of glycerine which is available in supermarket cake making aisles or chemists and leave to cool. Decant into cups or pots and use to blow bubbles with your elder bubble wands

What are we learning from this activity?
Mixing ingredients, chemistry, making resources.

Teasel Hedgehogs

Preparation needed: this is an activity for autumn and winter as you need the dead seed heads of the plant

Resources: gloves, scissors or secateurs small beads, and glue or pens

Age range: early years, primary, secondary, adult

Group size: any

Additional issues: teasel plants have prickly stems so take care when gathering

You will often see Teasel plants in grasslands, near ponds, in hedgerows and undisturbed land. They are tall plants with thorny stems and a cone like green flower head with little clusters of purple flowers. In winter the seed heads turn brown.

Wear gloves as teasel plants are prickly and gather some of the brown dried flower heads (Autumn/winter time) You will need secateurs to snip off the flower heads.

Either stick on small beads as the hedgehog's eyes and nose or use pens to draw them on. These make very lovely ornaments or very cute additions to a Christmas wreath.

What are we learning from this activity?
Using natural materials. Using tools, wearing PPE, making objects, thinking about the features of hedgehogs.

Stick Fairies

Preparation needed: gather resources. You may want to make sure that suitable sticks are available

Resources: sticks, felt tip pens, a knife or potato peeler, string, a bag of material bits, scissors

Age range: early years, primary, secondary, adult

Group size: any

Additional issues: when using tools please ensure that there is suitable and adequate supervision

With younger children green wood sticks for instance hazel poles about the thickness of an adult's finger are simple to peel the bark from with a potato peeler. When using tools please ensure that there is suitable and adequate supervision. You may want to lopper some fresh sticks in advance.

Using a potato peeler or knife, whittle a little bark from one end of the stick about the size of an adult thumb nail. Using felt tips draw on a face. If you do not wish to use tools you may want to use stick on googly eyes instead. Use some material to make clothes for your little person. To make it into a fairy find a couple of leaves and tie them onto your figure to make wings.

You may alternatively decide to make elves or superheroes using the material as cloaks. I have used this activity to make historic figures to extend classroom activities, survivors and figures to illustrate different stories told at the setting including the nativity story, Rama and Sita and Stickman.

What are we learning from this activity?
Using tools, making resources, health and safety, selecting natural and manmade materials to create an object, animistic play, imaginative play.

Bat Log

Preparation needed: gather resources, you may want to cut small logs in advance

Resources: a small log each black card, glue, scissors, pencil, white circular stickers and a black pen or googly eyes. (thick pole, bow saw, saw horse or fixing point to hold pole securely)

Age range: early years, primary, secondary, adult

Group size: any but if sawing close supervision is required

Additional issues: this activity can be extended for learners by letting them select and saw their own log which can be used as a good introduction to sawing. For the younger participants I like to make the first few groove in the log so that the saw blade has a good guide when the children use it

This is a good activity to use when learning about bats or alternatively you may want to use it for Halloween. Choose a log. Make sure that it has a flat edge so that it stands on one end. On a piece of black card, trace around your hands. Cut out the hand outlines and glue onto the back of the log to make the bat wings. Add on googly eyes or stickers made into eyes. Draw on a mouth. If you are doing this for Halloween, you may want to add some fangs to make it into a vampire bat!

Did you know that the collective noun for a group of bats is a colony? Most bats have eye sight as good as yours or mine but because they tend to fly at dusk (They are crepuscular animals ... I learnt this fact from my young son!) they use echo location to pinpoint their prey.

What are we learning from this activity?
Bat facts, drawing around shapes and scissor skills. Using natural materials and manmade materials to make an object.

Superhero Logs

Preparation needed: small log per child. You may want to pre-cut these in advance

Resources: paper, material, card, string, paint, pens, scissors, foil, shiny paper, glitter, glue, stickers, googly eyes, (thick pole, bow saw, saw horse or fixing point to hold pole securely. You may want a palm drill to add in arms)

Age range: early years, primary, secondary, adult

Group size: any, but if sawing close supervision is required

Additional issues: this activity can be extended for learners by letting them select and saw their own log which can be used as a good introduction to sawing

Think about superheroes and how you can make your own. Children may want to make a superhero they already know, or you may want to encourage them to invent their own using their own imagination to attribute super powers and skills to their logs. They make great discussion starters.

Choose a log suitable for your super hero. Make sure it has a flat base, so it can stand upright. Design the superheroes costume and accessories from craft materials provided by the teacher or natural materials you can find around you. You may want to use a drill, (palm or battery) and make holes to insert sticks or pipe cleaners for arms.

What are we learning from this activity?
This is a great activity for Superhero projects as well as good for introducing tool use. Speaking and listening skills and imaginative thinking about skills and super powers desirable in their hero. Encourages animistic play.

Log Homes

Preparation needed: collect some suitable logs. You may want to split them in advance

Resources: glue, string, paints, paper, card, natural materials, Billhook or axe, mallet

Age range: early years, primary

Group size: any, one split log per child

Additional issues: take care when using tools

When doing a topic on different types of homes this activity complements it well. Explore the children's previous knowledge of the topic and ask them to share the type of home they live in. Do they or anyone they know live in an unusual type of home like a caravan, a boat or a castle? You can make individual homes, villages, towns or city of houses or use as fairy homes. Can they make a home like theirs or would they like to make their dream home?

Split some logs using an axe or a billhook. Place the blade in the centre of the end of a log and hit with a mallet to split the log. This is good as a two-person job with one person holding the bladed tool and the other person using the mallet. Pull the two halves of the log apart so that you have 2 'houses' flat faces. Provide a range of art and craft materials and give the children the opportunity to design and decorate their log to make a house. You may want to use longer logs to make tower blocks or larger buildings. Give children the opportunity to make tree cookies to use as wheels if they want to portray a van or caravan.

What are we learning from this activity?
Using tools, working with others, learning about houses, buildings and homes, thinking about the common features of homes for example windows and doors as well as features which make our homes individual.

Woodland Skittles

Preparation needed: gather resources

Resources: axe or billhook and mallet, several logs about 6" diameter and 8-10" high, a knife, paints or felt tips to decorate

Age range: early years (with lots of support) primary, secondary, adult

Group size: small when using tools

Additional issues: observe good tool practice and establish a safe tool area

Place the log on a secure flat surface. Place the billhook on the flat face of the log so that the blade is along the diameter and passes through the centre of the circle. Strike the billhook with the mallet hard and split the log in half. Repeat on each half of the log to make quarters. You may want to leave the skittles basic like this and decorate with paints or felt tip pens. You may however decide that you want to make these fantastic resources using the knife you may want to carefully carve the log quarters to be woodland animals, birds or fantasy figures like elves and fairies. Leave the bottom surface of each skittle flat. Decorate with pens or paint. These make great individual figures for playing in the woods or a set can be used for a game of skittles. A cricket ball or Boule (from the French beach game) work well. The winner of the game is the person who knocks down the highest number of skittles in a set number of bowls. If you write numbers on each skittle you can also play an exciting addition game. The person with the highest score is the winner.

What are we learning from this activity?
Making our own resources using natural materials, tool safety, using tools, following safety rules, playing with others, hand eye coordination.

Kazoo

Preparation needed: coppice a pole about 2" in diameter with about 6-8" lengths per person

Resources: coppice poles, loppers, billhooks, mallets, knives, elastic bands, pencils

Age range: early years, primary, secondary, adult

Group size: small. Work in pairs with an adult supervising each pair

Additional issues: this activity also explores trusting others and following sequences and safety rules

Cut a length of wood (a soft wood that splits easily along its grain such as hazel or birch works well.) about 6-8" long making sure there are no offshoots as this will affect the grain of the wood.

Working with a friend, Stand the stick on its end and hold the billhook by the handle and balance the blade on the upright stick. Make sure that you are working on a firm surface. Position the blade over the centre of the stick. Make eye contact with your partner and when you are ready tell them and they need to hit the back of the billhook blade sharply with a mallet. This should split the stick down its length. Place both halves on the stick side by side. Using a pen or pencil draw two lines on the raw face of the split stick to divide it into three equal sections. Colour in the middle section. Then repeat on the other half of the stick. Using a knife and always working away from you lightly pare off the central section of wood to remove the pencil or pen marks from both sticks. Put the two halves of the stick back together again and you should be able to see a slither of daylight in the central section. Find a blade of grass and place between the two halves running along the grain of the wood. Hold in place with an elastic band at each end and blow through the gap in the central section and you should get a kazoo sound. if the sound is not very good try changing the blade of grass or removing a little more wood until you get a sound you are happy with. What can you play on your kazoo? Play 'name that tune' either individually or in groups. How about a kazoo choir?

What are we learning from this activity?

Making our own resources, tool safety, using tools, working with other people, trial and error, making music, working as part of a team.

Mallet

Preparation needed: gather resources

Resources: A suitable log which needs to be a small straight log about the length of your fore arm, elbow to wrist and about 15cm diameter, a bow saw or folding saw, a billhook and mallet, a whittling knife, sand paper if desired

Age range: primary, secondary, adult

Group size: 1 or 2 pupils to 1 adult

Additional issues: this is quite a lengthy activity and will take a full session or spread over 2 sessions to achieve a completed product

Find a suitable log which needs to be straight with no forks or off shoots about the length of your forearm and about 15 cms in diameter. Mark the mid points of the log and using a bowsaw saw a ring around the circumference of the log no deeper than about 4 cms. Stand the log on one end and using a billhook and mallet position the blade about 4 cm from the edge and hit the back of the blade with the mallet to split the wood. This should join up with the cut around the circumference. Go around the log removing the excess wood to form the mallet's handle. This is made easier if working with a partner. The partner holds the billhook in position. The other person strikes the back of the billhook with a mallet. Finish using a knife to pare off the wood to make the handle as smooth as possible. Finish off with sandpaper to make it smoother if desired. You can leave the bark on the head of the mallet or remove according to taste.

If you want to repeat and extend this activity when the mallet is finished place the mallet on its head and using a billhook split the head straight down on either side to make 2 flat faced pieces which when placed in position resume the look of the original mallet. Drill 2 holes through both pieces of wood and the body of the mallet where the handle meets the head. Thread string through one hole on a cut piece, then the body then the other piece (still resuming the original mallet shape. Take the string back through the other holes and tie the ends making sure that there is room for a little bit of movement. Holding the handle point downwards and flap vigorously so that the loose sides bang on the middle bit and you have made a clapper instrument.

What are we learning from this activity?
Using tools responsibly, making your own tools and resources, using natural materials, working with others.

Leaf Tree

Preparation needed: collect resources, lopper some 50p diameter sized elder sticks

Resources: pencils or whittled sticks the size and length of a pencil, a thumb length piece of fresh elder or a yogurt pot filled with soil

Age range: early years, primary, secondary, adult

Group size: any

Additional issues: if using tools for whittling and lopping please ensure that you have correct ratios and follow your tool safe use policies. Be aware of sharpened points on sticks or pencils

Put a pencil or sharpened stick into a base with the point facing up. This can be a yogurt pot filled with soil or a block of elder branch with the pencil pushed into the soft pith.

Push a selection of leaves onto the pencil to build up a tree shape. Start with larger leaves at the bottom and graduate up to smallest leaves at the top to form a tree shape.

If you are doing this activity near Christmas use green leaves like ivy and drizzle over some PVA glue and glitter or sequins for a festive feel. You can buy environmentally friendly versions from craft shops and from online shops

What are we learning from this activity?
Fine motor skills, whittling skills, tool safety, personal artwork using natural resources, choosing and selecting resources, colours, shades, using nature as inspiration for craft activities, threading, sticking and decorating.

Woodland Cricket Bat

Preparation needed: gather resources

Resources: log, mallet, billhook, saw, knife, pine cones

Age range: older primary, secondary, adult

Group size: 1 or 2 to make the bat and a larger group to play the game

Additional issues: this activity requires a lot of supervision and time but makes a great project for older children interested in sports.

Find a log or branch about the diameter and length of an adult's lower leg. Using a billhook and mallet, split the log in half lengthways right down the centre to form the flat face of the bat. Using one half of the split log, mark the log into thirds. Saw a couple of centimetres in from the edge at the third mark, (excluding the flat face of the split log) Using a billhook and mallet carefully remove the wood to the saw mark from the top third of the bat to form the handle. Shape further with a knife as required. If there is plenty of time the bat can be smoothed further with sandpaper to give a smoother finish.

Now you can play a woodland cricket match with either a soft ball or pine cones.

What are we learning from this activity?
Making resources from natural materials, using a range of tools, adapting a well-known game to play with the resources around us.

Tree Cookie Dominoes

Preparation needed: gather resources

Resources: saw, saw horse, pens, paint (at least 6 different characters)

Age range: early years, primary, secondary, adult

Group size: small

Additional issues: close supervision is required when children are using a bowsaw

Cut as many tree cookies as you can, 30+ is ideal. Draw a line through the diameter and paint each half a different colour. Try to have at least 5 or 6 different colours to make the game more challenging.

Alternatively, you could make dominos to suit different topics you are covering in your sessions, how about drawing on different leaf shapes, bugs, animals, seeds, or even story characters to make individualised sets for your children. Divide each disc in two and draw pictures on both halves.

The Idea of the game is to match the colour (or picture) to another disc with the same colour (or picture). This is also great for imaginative play, encouraging children to make up their own game rules and pattern making. Try adding in a few discs with a different colour in each quarter instead of each half.

What are we learning from this activity?
Colours, matching, working with others, making up rules, following rules.

Tree Cookie Pairs

Preparation needed: gather resources

Resources: saw, saw horse, pens, natural materials, glue, varnish

Age range: early years, primary

Group size: small

Additional issues: when using varnish please make sure it is suitable for children's toys

Cut tree cookies 20+ is ideal. Either draw or stick on natural materials on each tree cookie, for example leaves, seed cases, animal prints, flowers or pictures of local wildlife. Make sure you have 2 of each type. Varnish to protect and leave to dry.

Place all the tree cookies decorated face down and take it in turns to turn over two of the discs. If you find a matching pair, you win them. The winner is the person with the most tree cookies at the end of the game.

If you have or know someone with a Band Saw it is possible to make a large quantity of tree cookies for activities in a fraction of the time it would take to hand saw them.

What are we learning from this activity?
Matching, working with others, turn taking, following rules.

Footprint Cookies

Preparation needed: gather resources

Resources: log, bowsaw, paints or pens

Age range: early years, primary

Group size: any

Additional issues: you can seal the painted foot print cookies with varnish to preserve them and make them a great reusable resource

Saw lots of tree cookies. Paint on foot prints on each cookie and leave to dry. Set a trail of tree cookie foot prints and let the children follow them. Why not have a teddy or cuddly toy at the end of the trail for the children to find.

If you want to print little human feet onto these discs scrunch up your hand into a fist. Dip your fist (the flat little finger side) into paint and carefully press onto the disc. This looks like a little foot print. Add on toe prints using finger tips or cotton buds to complete and leave to dry before varnishing if you want to make these a permanent resource.

What are we learning from this activity?
Sawing skills, painting, health and safety, laying a trail. Following a trail, working with friends.

Stick and Wire Christmas Tree

Preparation needed: gather resources

Resources: loppers, hand drill or palm drill, wire (I use floristry wire) wire cutters, scissors, beads or elder, straight freshly cut sticks, pine cones

Age range: early years, primary, secondary, adult

Group size: small as supervision is needed for tool use

Additional issues: when drilling you may want to use clamps to keep each stick still and give you something to hold especially with the shorter sticks and beads

Choose a range of sticks in graduating lengths. Arrange into a triangle shape. Using a palm drill or hand drill, make a hole all the way through midway along the stick. Thread a length of wire through the longest stick then thread on a large bead. Thread on the next longest stick followed by another bead and so on until you end up with the smallest piece at the top. You may want to use readymade beads in festive colours or alternatively make your own elder beads by lopping a fresh length of elder at least the diameter of a one penny piece. Lop the elder into short lengths and remove the soft pith in the centre of the stick. I find a tent peg very useful for this job. You can leave the bark on or easily peel it off if you prefer. It is possible to use felt tip pens to decorate the handmade beads. You can also make beads by cutting short pieces of wood (Hazel works well) and drilling a hole through each piece.

Fashion a hanging loop from the wire and thread it back through the top piece of wood to secure. Decorate with ribbon. Hang up to display. It can be displayed flat against a wall or suspended so the sticks can be pushed around to make a 3D tree.

You can also make this tree using sisal string to tie the sticks together instead of wire.

What are we learning from this activity?
Using tools, making an object, using natural and manmade materials, celebration of festivals.

Tree Cookie Blackboards

Preparation needed: gather resources

Resources: a medium sized log, saw horse or fixing point, bow saw, blackboard paint, paint brush, chalks, hand drill, string, scissors

Age range: early years, primary, secondary, adult

Group size: small with supervision

Additional issues: none

Modern white boards are often seen in classrooms as a learning tool but what about outside? Try making this old fashioned natural alternative. They also make lovely presents to take home.

Secure a log and cut a slice using a bowsaw. Using a drill, make a couple of holes at the top of the slice. Paint one side of the slice with specialised blackboard paint, (available in most DIY shops) and leave to dry. Thread a string through the holes at the top of the slice to hang the chalk board for display. Use as a learning resource for class answers, mark making, mud kitchen recipes, forest shop signs, reminders and treasure hunt clues.

What are we learning from this activity?
Using tools, using natural materials, making our own resources. Mark making, literacy and writing.

Natural Wall Hanging

Preparation needed: gather resources

Resources: Loose weave Hessian, a whittling knife, a stick, natural materials

Age range: early years, primary, secondary, adult

Group size: any

Additional issues: be careful with pointed sticks and lop of the tops before leaving the area

Give each participant a piece of hessian or alternatively you may want to create a group piece of work. Using a knife carefully whittle a stick to a sharp point. Gather a range of natural materials such as grasses, flowers with stalks, reeds, feathers, lichens, leaves and twigs, and using the pointed stick, gently ease the hessian fibres apart to make a hole and carefully poke the natural materials through the hessian. Build up the hanging and display by attaching to a straight stick with string or staples, glue or sewing.

What are we learning from this activity?
Using natural materials to make a work of art, making tools to help us complete a task.

Mushroom

Preparation needed: gather resources

Resources: a suitable log which needs to be a small straight log about the length of your fore arm, elbow to wrist and about 20cm diameter, a bow saw or folding saw, a whittling knife, sand paper if desired

Age range: older primary, secondary, adult

Group size: small

Additional issues: none

Mark the mid points of the log and using a bowsaw saw a ring around the circumference of the log no deeper than about 5 cms. Stand the log on its side and secure so it does not roll. Using the saw cut a shallow wedge from base to the cut leaving the base as wide as possible. Turn the log 45 degrees and repeat. Do this another couple of times and it will look a bit like a table lamp. Using the knife remove more of the 'mushroom stem' to shape it. When you are happy with the lower part, stand the mushroom on its base and using the saw cut off the corners around the top and use the knife to shape. Fashion the mushroom cap to any shape you desire and sand to finish off.

These look lovely painted or left natural and are great for decoration or as a play resource. Let children include these in small people play, as a prop in fairy land for stick fairies or as a display resource.

What are we learning from this activity?
Using tools responsibly, making your own decoration and resources, using natural materials.

Elder Beads

Preparation needed: locate an elder tree in need of pruning or bring onto site fresh elder sticks

Resources: loppers, folding saw, tent pegs, felt tips, cotton string

Age range: early years, primary, secondary, adult

Group size: any

Additional issues: care must be taken when using sharp tools. Do not press out the pith into the palm of your hand. The elder tree is thought by many to be magical so please thank the tree for letting you have some of its branches (just in case!) A certain boy wizard's wand was made of elder with a phoenix feather core

Cut some elder sticks about the diameter of a 10p piece. Lopper into pieces about 3-4cms long. The centre of the elder stick is pithy and can easily be pushed out with a tent peg.

The elder bark is easily removed by peeling it off. Leave the bead to dry off for a few minutes then you can decorate the beads with felt tip pens or permanent markers. Thread onto cotton string to make bracelets or necklaces. These make lovely natural presents for Mother's Day.

What are we learning from this activity?
The identification and properties of elder, making decorative items, present making, using tools.

Peashooters

Preparation needed: locate an elder tree in need of pruning or bring onto site fresh elder sticks

Resources: loppers, folding saw, tent pegs

Age range: older primary, secondary, adult

Group size: any

Additional issues: care must be taken when using sharp tools. Do not press out the pith into the palm of your hand. The elder tree is thought by many to be magical so please thank the tree for letting you have some of its branches (just in case!). When using the peashooter never suck, only blow. Never fire at other people, especially to the face area

Cut some elder sticks about the diameter of a 10p piece. Lopper into pieces about 8cms long. The centre of the elder stick is pithy and can easily be pushed out with a tent peg. Make sure there are no junctions or knots on your length as the pith will fork inside the stick. Blow through the tube to make sure it is clear. Ammo can be fresh peas, dried peas or chewed pieces of paper. Set up a target and get practicing.

The elder bark is easily removed by peeling it off. Leave the stick to dry off for a few minutes then you can decorate the peashooters with felt tip pens or permanent markers, do not use felt tip pens around the blow end or the children could end up with purple lips!

What are we learning from this activity?
The identification and properties of elder, making decorative items, present making, using tools.

Marionette Puppets

Preparation needed: make Elder beads and tree cookies

Resources: loppers, folding saw, tent pegs, felt tips, string, palm drill or hand drill, sticks

Age range: early years, primary, secondary, adult

Group size: small

Additional issues: care must be taken when using sharp tools. Do not press out the pith into the palm of your hand. The elder tree is thought by many to be magical so please thank the tree for letting you have some of its branches (just in case!) The Elder tree quite likes having its branches trimmed and shoots fresh poles at cut sites the following year

Cut a few tree cookies, preferably one with a smaller diameter for a head and a larger diameter for the body. Drill 2 holes in head cookie, one at the top and one at the bottom. Drill 5 holes in the body cookie, one for the neck and one for each of the limbs.

Cut some elder sticks about the diameter of a 10p piece. Lopper into pieces about 3-4cms long. The centre of the elder stick is pithy and can easily be pushed out with a tent peg. Tie a bead onto the end of a string for a shoe. Thread on some elder beads for the legs and attach to the body. Repeat with the other limbs. Attach the body to the head with a piece of string.

Make a cross from a couple of sticks. Run a string from the top of the head to the centre of the stick. Tie a string from the hands to opposite sides of the cross. Waggle the cross from side to side to wave the arms. For younger children this will be enough.

Take another stick and tie strings from the centre of each leg (the knees) to each end of the second stick. Work the legs by tilting the stick to lift the knees and make a stripping motion. With a bit of practice, you can make your puppets move and interact with each other. Why not make up a play together or take your puppets for a walk around your outdoor site.

For younger children you can make the puppets but do not add the strings, so they can use them as dolls or woodland babies for pretend play.

What are we learning from this activity?

The identification and properties of elder, making and working marionette puppets, using tools.

Leaf Bash Bunting

Preparation needed: pre-cut material triangles (cotton-based material works best)

Resources: pre-cut material triangles, string, mallets, flat surface (playgrounds, paths and log seats work well) leaves and flowers

Age range: early years, primary, secondary, adult

Group size: any

Additional issues: ask younger children to hold the mallet with 2 hands to ensure that they do not hit their fingers with it

Use cotton-based material to make this bunting. Collect a range of deciduous leaves from trees and ground plants, the juicier the better! Stinging nettles work really well but please wear gloves when picking and handling leaves. Buttercup and pink campion petals as well as dandelions and garden flowers add lots of colour to your bunting.

Arrange your leaves and petals on half of the triangle and carefully fold it over. Using the mallet bang the material until the colours of the leaves and petals have transferred onto the material. Pick the residue organic matter off the material and display.

This activity of bashing leaves and flowers is also known as Hapa Zome.

To display the bunting, tie loop some string around a tree or fence post. Double it so you have 2 strings of equal length and twist them together many times to make one string then secure the string to another point. Poke two of the triangles corners into the twists of the string. This is very effective unless it is very windy when you might prefer to use clothes pegs or staples to secure. Use this activity alongside the mud painting bunting.

What are we learning from this activity?
Using tools, selecting and using natural resources, making a decorative item.

6

Fire activities

Fire Making

Practice lighting fires before you do it during the session so that you are confident.

The key to successful fire lighting is preparation. Ensure you have everything you need before you start.

Decide what you will use to make a spark – matches or fire strikes are effective. Using a lighter can lead to burns as the metal can get hot. Using a bow drill is very interesting and a great session to use with older children and young people but if you are not sufficiently practiced at getting it to work in a reasonably quick time, it is not really a spectator sport! You need a quick and effective method especially when you are working with very young children. Practice making fires correctly, but it is also worth knowing the cheats way of making fire (just in case you ever need it)

Make sure you have plenty of tinder to build up and start the fire. You can use dried grass, dried nettle stalks, dried gorse, dried pine needles, birch bark, and wood shavings. If you are in need of some emergency tinder there are other things that you may have in your kit that you can use. For instance, you can use char cloth, cotton wool, (I like to use cotton wool makeup removal pads as they can be split in half and fluffed up to catch sparks), tumble dryer fluff, unused teabags, shredded tissues, paper (old bus tickets, lesson plans), dressings from a first aid kit or even fluffed up tampons in times of desperation!

I often carry a pre-prepared tinder bundle in a zip lock bag in my rucksack during wet weather that I know will make fire no matter what!

In damp weather you may need something to get your fire going initially. I often carry a couple of individually wrapped fire lighters that can be placed in the tinder pile to ensure success. If you do not have those there are some other things that can be used alcohol hand gel, petroleum jelly, this can be in the form of a chapped lips stick or in a tub or tin (make a cotton wool and petroleum jelly sandwich as a DIY fire lighter) and some crisps for instance Pringles burn for a prolonged time (use individually and whole) so it could be worth raiding some packed lunch boxes if you are desperate.

Lumps of charcoal from previous fires will catch fire easily so it is good to find some charcoal bits to add to your preparation pile.

Why not make the preparation part of the activity? Ask the children to each bring you 10 dry sticks each as thick as the lead inside a pencil. The sticks need to be 'dry and snappy' rather than 'green and bendy'. They could then be asked to bring another 10 sticks each as thick as their fingers and thumbs, another 10 as thick as their wrists and maybe find one each as thick as their leg.

Make piles or sticks close to the fire area and have handfuls of thin sticks within a hands reach of where you are working.

To make a small fire you will need to make a raft platform

of dried sticks about the thickness of your thumb laid side by side. Place your tinder bundle on top of this. Build a tepee style structure around the bundle using the thinnest twigs you can find. Put slightly thicker sticks around the tepee. Light the match or fire strike close to the kindling by striking it away from your body. Carefully add sticks onto the fire starting with the thinnest sticks first to feed it with fuel. If the fire is not burning very well, try blowing on it or wafting it to introduce more oxygen.

Keep feeding your fire with fuel once it is lit.

If the fire does not catch, try blowing on it gently or wafting it to introduce more oxygen to help reignite it.

Once the fire is lit do not leave it unattended.

When you want to put the fire out stop feeding it fuel and allow the fire to go to a smoulder.

Once this has happened sprinkle water over the fire to stop the smoulder.

When you are sure the fire is out and the remains are cold pick up the remains and dispose of responsibly. Nobody should be able to see that you have lit a fire there

Camp Fire Cookery

When cooking outdoors it is important that you risk assess the area and the activity.

You need to apply food hygiene regulations to ensure food safety. It is important that you ensure that a high standard of cleanliness and hygiene is maintained at all times. Keep hands clean when cooking and handling food. Use antiseptic wipes or soap and water. The best way to remove bacteria from your hands is by using running water. Dry your hands well using paper towels. Ensure that you clean your hands before and after handling food, after going to the toilet, sneezing, coughing or blowing you nose. If you are using gloves to prepare food, they are the same as your hands and you need to wash them before using them and in between if necessary. Wear clean clothes where possible.

Cooking destroys bacteria that can cause food poisoning. You must ensure that food is thoroughly cooked through. Do not cook any meat on the bone and split open and ensure it is cooked inside as well as outside before eating.

Keep cooked foods and raw foods separate from each other and be careful to avoid cross contamination.

Ensure that all cooking pots, pans and utensils are clean before you use them. You can make sure that things do not get dirty or contaminated when out before using them to cook by covering them in cling film or putting into a sealed bag.

If you are cooking using a stick, for example toasting marshmallows or bannock, use a green stick and remove the bark.

Store food in cool boxes and keep raw and cooked foods separate. Keep food covered wherever possible to help prevent bacteria as well as birds, insects and hungry squirrels from stealing your food.

Think of ways to cook or prepare foods that cut down on handling, for instance mixing in a zip lock bag, using tongs.

When you have cooked food, it should be eaten as soon as possible. Do not reheat it!

Make sure that cuts and sores are covered with a waterproof dressing. If on the hand, once the waterproof dressing is on wear disposable gloves to give added protection but remember to wash as hands.

Wash hands before eating.

Nettle Crisps

Preparation needed: this is an activity which requires a fire

Resources: fire, pan with a cup of cooking oil, fresh nettle leaves, tongs or draining spoon, metal rack, a sprinkle of salt if desired

Age range: early years, primary, secondary, adult delicious whatever your age but probably better to only allow older ones and adults to prepare

Group size: any

Additional issues: be aware that this is an activity that should be closely supervised by a responsible adult as oil and fire are a combustible combination, also picking nettles can also be a bit ouchy so gloves are recommended. (When this oil has cooled down, it can be reused in the seed bombing activity)

Gather some fresh nettle leaves, the spring/early summer ones are the best quality. Wear gloved when picking to avoid being stung. On the camp fire heat a frying pan or saucepan with a few centimetres depth of oil. Make sure that this is on a stable base to avoid being knocked over. Drop nettle leaves into the oil for a few seconds, fish the leaves out and place on a piece of kitchen roll or a metal cooling tray to drain. Eat when cool. If you like sprinkle with salt, black pepper or paprika according to taste when still warm. How about experimenting with a range of leaves?

Clover, dandelion, plantain, wood sorrel, beech leaves, hawthorn and wild garlic may be good to start with. Please only try leaves that you can easily identify, and you are sure are edible.

What are we learning from this activity?
Using natural resources, foraging, cooking on a camp fire, exploring taste.

Pancakes

Preparation needed: camp fire, gather resources

Resources: 200g of flour, 4 large eggs, 600 ml of milk, butter or sunflower oil, large frying pan, large spatula, plate to serve, fillings (see ideas below)

Age range: early years, primary, secondary, adult

Group size: any

Additional issues: take care when cooking over the fire and always clean hands before cooking and eating

Prepare pancake mix by putting the flour in a bowl, crack in the eggs and add about a third of the milk. I use a hand mixer (the turn the handle variety) so children can join in too. Gradually add in the rest of the milk and the mixture should be smooth.

Heat a frying pan on the fire and melt a knob of butter or sunflower oil if you prefer. You can either make large individual pancakes or when I use my big paella pan I make about 4 small ones at a time. When the pancake has cooked for about a minute or so flip it over using a large spatula. (It should be golden brown in colour) Cook the other side and pop it on a plate. There are many ways you can serve pancakes. Fill with grated cheese, salad or even a warmed hotdog. My son likes a bit of butter melted on the hot pancake with a light sprinkling of sugar. I like to add a sprinkle of cinnamon to mine. In autumn warmed blackberries or stewed apples and sugar is lovely.

If I have lots of children, you can make many pancakes and stack them on a plate just popping them back into the pan to warm before filling and serving. To serve if you do not have enough camp plates, you can get paper plates and fold them into a cone to hold the pancakes. Start making a collection of wooden fish and chip shop forks (you can buy these wholesale) then there is no washing up!

What are we learning from this activity?

Using the camp fire for cooking, following a recipe, eating together as a group, changing states, if this is done around Easter time you can explore cultural foods. If you fill with seasonal fruit you can link with foraging and where food comes from.

Elder Flower Fritters

Preparation needed: camp fire, gather resources

Resources: 100g of flour, 2 large eggs, 300 ml of milk, sunflower oil, frying pan, large spatula, plates to serve, icing sugar

Age range: early years, primary, secondary, adult

Group size: any

Additional issues: take care when cooking over the fire and always clean hands before cooking and eating

Make up the batter mix. Take 15 large elderflower heads. Look for the fresh ones rather than when the flowers are starting to brown. Tap and shake the heads a few times to dislodge any minibeasts hiding there. You can wash with water and pat dry.

Heat a pan on the camp fire and put in enough oil to be about 1 cm deep. When the oil is hot dip a flower head into the batter mix and shake off any excess. Don't worry if it clumps together and looks a bit sad. Pop it into the hot oil and cook until it has become flower shaped again and is a golden brown. Remove and drain. Sprinkle with icing sugar and serve warm. You can add a little cinnamon to taste.

You can also use the batter to make apple fritters. Core an apple and slice into rings, toss in a little flour then dip in the batter mix and fry. One day with some spare batter we made biscuit fritters with a packet of hobnobs and very nice they were too.

What are we learning from this activity?
Cooking outdoors, Using foraged ingredients, experimental cookery.

Orchard Parcels

Preparation needed: gather resources

Resources: chopping board, knife, foil, orchard fruits, (apples, pears, plums), brown sugar, cinnamon, sultanas, marshmallows

Age range: early years, primary, secondary, adult

Group size: small

Additional issues: Ensure hands and surfaces are clean. Providing hand washing facilities when cooking outside. Close supervision when participants are using a knife

Cut up the fruit into large chunks ensuring that all pips and stones are removed. Place the chopped fruit into the centre of a large foil square. Sprinkle on a teaspoon of sugar, a quarter teaspoon of cinnamon, a table spoon of sultanas and a few marshmallows if desired. Wrap the parcel over and place in the embers of the fire to bake. Take care when serving as it will be hot. For a bit of extra decadence take a pot of Cornish clotted cream with you to serve.

What are we learning from this activity?
Preparing and cooking food outside, using different cooking methods, camp fire safety, healthy foods, health and hygiene.

Corn on The Cob

Preparation needed: camp fire, gather resources

Resources: cobs of corn, tin foil, butter, pointed sticks, bread knife, chopping board, camp fire

Age range: early years, primary, secondary, adult

Group size: any

Additional issues: make sure the corn has sufficiently cooled before eating to prevent burning the mouth

There are two ways to cook corn over a camp fire. The first method is to wrap a corn cob in foil with a smear of butter and place in the embers of the fire for 10-15 minutes turning occasionally. The second method is great for children to cook their own snack. Using a bread knife, saw a corn on the cob into thick slices 4/5 kernels thick, Press onto a sharpened stick and hold above the embers of the fire to toast for 10 minutes then eat from the stick when sufficiently cooled. You can spread a little butter on the kernels if you like it that way.

You can also prepare Jacket potatoes and sweet potatoes on the fire by wrapping in foil and cooking in the embers. They will take longer ½ to 1 ½ hours depending on their size. Make sure you prick them with a fork prior to cooking and turn them frequently using tongs.

What are we learning from this activity?
Preparing a snack, eating natural food. Cooking over a campfire.

Making your own butter

Preparation needed: gather resources. I often buy the cream when it is reduced in the supermarket and pop it in the freezer, taking it out before going to the woods so it has a few hours to defrost

Resources: a clean jam jar with lid or plastic container with tight fitting lid. Double cream, water, a bowl, a little salt, spoon, knife to spread

Age range: early years, primary, secondary, adult

Group size: small

Additional issues: make sure your hands are clean before handling the butter. You may want to have several jars at one time and let everybody have a shake, passing the jar when their arms are tired

Half fill a jam jar with double cream, put on the lid and shake vigorously for 5-10 minutes until the cream has gone solid and there is some liquid separated in the jar. Pour out the liquid (you could use this to make waffles or scones if you are feeling creative)

Remove the formed butter from the jar using the spoon. Make it into a ball and rinse well in the water squishing it a bit as you go. Mix in salt to taste.

Spread on corn, toast, bread or crumpets. If you have any butter left it can be refrigerated and will last for a week.

What are we learning from this activity?
Science – changing states, irreversible reactions, exploring the process of how butter is made, participating in a task to achieve a result, tasting the fruits of our labours, working with others, taking turns.

Garlic Bread

Preparation needed: gather resources

Resources: a French bread Baguette, butter (see previous recipe), a chopping board, a knife, wild garlic leaves and flowers, fried onion and cheese to taste (not necessary but a nice addition) Tin foil

Age range: early years, primary, secondary, adult

Group size: any

Additional issues: make sure your hands are clean before preparing or eating food. You may want to have more than one baguette depending on the size of the group

This is a delicious snack or an accompaniment for any campfire meal. Unroll a very long piece of foil and prepare the bread on it by almost cutting through the baguette in slices but not quite going through the base. Collect wild garlic leaves and flowers (rinse well with water and pat dry in a tea towel) and chop very finely. If you do not have wild garlic in your area or it is the wrong time of year, you can use some crushed garlic paste (get it in tubes or jars from the supermarket or use fresh garlic cloves finely chopped. Mix with the butter. If you are not using butter you have just made but the shop bought variety make sure it is not chilled and is soft. Mix the chopped wild garlic with the butter. If you are using fried (cooled) onions and grated cheese mix this in to bowl at this point and spread a spoonful of mixture in each slice of baguette. Wrap well in the foil and place in the embers of the fire for a few minutes until the butter and cheese have melted and the bread is warmed through. Remove from fire and unwrap. Break the baguette into the slices and serve.

What are we learning from this activity?
Preparing and cooking food using a campfire, food hygiene skills, eating food from other countries, exploring different cultures, foraging and using fresh ingredients

Winter Garland Bird Feeder

Preparation needed: camp fire, gather resources

Resources: 2 metal sieves, wire, wire cutters, long stick, unpopped popcorn, cranberries, thick needles (tapestry or binca needles work well), strong cotton, camp fire

Age range: early years, primary, secondary, adult

Group size: any

Additional issues: this is a good camp fire activity especially for winter solstice or Christmas celebrations. Come back to the camp area at a later stage and remove the cotton thread

Wire together 2 metal sieves of the same size to form a sphere. Bind one of the sieve handles to a long sturdy stick. Put a handful of unpopped popcorn kernels into the sieves and using the long stick, hold over an established (low flame, lots of embers) camp fire. Gently shake the sieves and you will see the corn kernels start to pop. When the majority of them have popped remove from the heat and tip into a bowl to cool. You could try eating some of them, they have a lovely smoky flavour.

Cut a long thread about a metre to 1½ metres long of cotton and tie a knot about 20 cms in from the end. Thread the needle at the other end and thread on popcorn to make a lovely white garland with which to decorate your outdoor area alternating the popcorn with cranberries can give a very festive feel. Try other dried fruits like sultanas or dried apple and make a winter feast for the birds in your outdoor area.

Please make sure that you revisit the outdoor area to remove the cotton thread at a later stage once the birds have enjoyed their winter treat.

What are we learning from this activity?
Sewing, threading, changing states, camp fire cooking, caring for wildlife, winter celebrations.

Savoury Rice

Preparation needed: camp fire, gather resources, you may want to prepare some of the ingredients before hand and place in zip lock bags or containers to take to the site with you

Resources: camp fire, flat based large frying pan (I use a paella pan), a spatula, a flask of boiling water or a kettle or storm kettle to boil water on site. A little olive or sunflower oil. Rice, grated carrots, a handful of sweetcorn and peas, a courgette, tomatoes, chopped onion, mushrooms, peppers (add or subtract vegetables to taste) a couple of stock cubes (vegetable or chicken) You can also add chopped bacon, chicken, pepperoni, cut up frankfurter sausages or ham if you want a meaty dish, a mug, a chopping board and a grater

Age range: early years, primary, secondary, adult

Group size: any

Additional issues: Make sure you have washed and dried your hands before starting. I like to pre chop the onions and courgette and grate the carrots prior to the session and take them with me but they can be prepared on site if you like

This can be a vegan dish or meaty depending on your choice of ingredients.

Prepare the vegetables making sure everything is finely chopped. Grate carrots or slither in thin slices with a vegetable peeler, If young children are helping I like to pop some cherry tomatoes or mushrooms in a cup and give them clean safety scissors to snip them into tiny pieces.

Heat a little oil in the pan on the fire and fry the vegetables (and meat if you are using it) until cooked. Fill up a mug with rice (I like Basmati but use what you have) add to the pan and stir. Crumble the stock cubes into the same mug and fill up with hot water. Stir and pour in the pan. Then fill up the mug with hot water again and add to the pan. Simmer on the fire until all the liquid is absorbed by the rice. You may need to add a little more water if the rice is a bit hard. Wild garlic leaves finely chopped taste nice in this. You may want to add some seasoning to taste.

Lovely served with garlic or Flat bread. Can be eaten hot or cold.

Magic Soup Story

Preparation needed: camp fire, gather resources, you may want to prepare some of the ingredients beforehand especially if doing this activity with young children and place in lidded containers to take to the site with you

Resources: camp fire, flat based large pan (I use a large stock pot but if you have a cauldron or a Dutch oven that would be fantastic) a spatula, a flask of boiling water or a kettle or storm kettle to boil water on site. A little olive or sunflower oil. Chopped carrots, potatoes, sweet potatoes, parsnip, swede, a handful of sweetcorn and peas, a courgette, tomatoes, chopped onion, mushrooms, peppers, any other vegetables you can have to hand, a handful of red lentils if you want (add or subtract vegetables to taste) a couple of stock cubes (vegetable) a chopping board, a knife. A large bag with the containers with prepared vegetables in and another bag with whole vegetables in it. Bowls and spoons

Age range: early years, early primary

Group size: any

Additional issues: make sure you have washed and dried your hands before starting. I like to pre-chop the ingredients and pop them into lidded containers or zip lock bags prior to the session and take them with me but they can be prepared on site if you like. Also take whole vegetables so the children can see them before preparation

This is a lovely activity which is part storytelling, role play, drama and part cookery which teaches children about a variety of vegetables, healthy food, working cooperatively and sharing. I like to do this as the end of children's time with me on a forest school programme as part of a feast session.

This activity works well with two adults, one as the story teller and one as the magic soup maker.

Ask the children to sit around the fire, rub your tummy and tell them you are so hungry. Open the vegetable bag and hand around the whole vegetables explaining what they are as you go. Explain to the children you have all these vegetables, but you don't know how to make them into something on the fire.

The other adult (The soup maker) arrives on the scene carrying a large cooking pot and a closed bag of prepared ingredients. The Soup maker places the pot on the ground, takes off the lid and with a ladle pretends to take a sip of the soup and frowns.

The leader asks what they are doing and asks what is wrong. The soup maker then explains they are eating magic soup but there is something wrong with it, it doesn't taste right, and it needs an extra ingredient. He/she asks the children if anyone happens to have an onion with them. When the child offers the onion the soup maker makes a show of putting it into the magic bag says some magic words and asks the children to make chop chop, chop motions with their hands. The Soup maker then whips the prepared onion out of the bag and puts it into the pot pretending to stir it. The soup maker then pretends to taste the soup and says, "still something is missing – does anyone have a potato/carrot/ parsnip etc and when they are offered them puts them into the bag and returns with the prepared ingredients each time asking the children to 'chop' them up. When the ingredients are in the pot the leader says I have some extra ingredients with me and pops a bit of oil into the pan and sticks the pot on the fire stirring occasionally. When hot add a flask or two of boiling water or water previously heated on the fire and let it simmer for half an hour or so while the children complete an activity away from the fire, leaving the soup maker to tend to their soup. Whilst the children are away, add in a few stock cubes and let it cook well. You can add in a handful of lentils or some cornflour mixed with a little water to thicken if you like. Get out bowls (or paper cups) and spoons and make sure the magic bag is unexplorable! When the soup is ready the leader should ask the children to return to the fire when the leader asks if they can try some of the soup. The soup maker offers bowls of soup to all the children to try as they have helped to make it by supplying lots of flavoursome vegetables and a bit of magic to make it. Ask the children to see if they can taste their ingredient in the soup. Talk about sharing and working together to make the feast and how nice it is to achieve something together as a team. Over acting on the part of the adults always goes down well with the children.

What are we learning from this activity?

Storytelling, talking and listening, imagination, sharing, using healthy ingredients, extending vocabulary and knowledge of vegetables. cooking together and using magic. Children, even the most fussy eaters will often try this soup because they have had a part in the story. If you want to read a story to the children as they eat their soup, stories such as Olivers Vegetables by Vivian French or the Hot Stone Soup traditional tale work well.

Flat Bread

Preparation needed: camp fire, gather resources

Resources: camp fire, flat based frying pan, a bowl, a spatula or tongs, a clean tea towel to place the finished breads on. 300 g of plain or wholemeal flour, ¼ tsp of salt, 150 mls of tepid water and 3 tbsps. of olive or sunflower oil. You will also need some more oil for cooking

Age range: early years, primary, secondary, adult

Group size: any

Additional issues: make sure you have washed and dried your hands before starting

Place flour and salt in the bowl and gradually add in the water. Mix well to make a soft dough then add in the oil and knead for 5 minutes. If the dough is too dry add a little more water, if it is too sticky add a little more flour. When the dough is kneaded leave to stand for about half an hour.

This first part can be done in the classroom before venturing out and popped into a covered box if that is easier.

When your campfire has gone past its initial burn and is glowing hot but with fewer flames divide the dough into small apple sized pieces and flatten either with hands or using a rolling pin on a plate sprinkled with a little flour to ensure it does not stick.

Heat a large, flat bottomed frying pan – I use a paella pan on the fire, so we can do lots at once. Place a little oil in the pan and swish it around to cover the whole surface. Cook each flat bread for about 2 minutes on each side flipping with tongs or a spatula. Remove and place on a tea towel or plate until cool enough to handle and serve with dips, jam, honey, humus or spread with mashed fruit or as an accompaniment with soup.

What are we learning from this activity?

Preparing and cooking food outside, seeing the process of following a recipe to make a completed product, food hygiene and fire safety. The social side of eating as a group.

Low Ropes Challenge

Preparation needed: set up course in advance, check surrounding ground for sharp sticks and rocks

Resources: thick ropes, Slack lines, carpet tiles or off cuts

Age range: early years, primary, secondary, adult

Group size: small

Set up a low rope and slack line between two trees. Make sure that the rope/line will have enough clearance even when a child is standing on it of about 10-20 cms. Use Carpet tiles or carpet off cuts wrapped around the trees where the rope or slack lines touch the tree so as to not damage the bark. Tie another line to the tree at child shoulder height for the children to hold onto as they move across the rope. Make sure that you again protect the bark from rope burns. If you have older children, you may want to do without the hand rope so they can practice their balancing skills further. I am still at the stage where I need long sticks to hold on to but some amazing teenagers I worked with were balancing on the slack lines one on one foot and jumping and landing like professional tightrope walkers!

What are we learning from this activity?
Improving balancing skills, problem solving, gross motor development, taking turns, encouraging others.

Lily Pads

Preparation needed: none

Resources: 2 ropes and sit mats

Age range: primary, secondary, adult

Group size: any

Additional issues: simplify for younger children

For this game you need two ropes or natural features to represent the banks of a river. The goal is to have the group cross the river. Give each group of 4 or 5 members 6 or 7 sit mats or 'Lily Pads' (more if you want to make the challenge simpler.

They need to cross the river. Each 'lily pad will only support two feet and one hand at a time, any more than this and the lily pad will sink. (if a mat is overweight the leader removes the mat from the group) also any mats left unattended for a few seconds it will float away and will be removed by the leader. If anyone in the group touches the water, the team must start again.

What are we learning from this activity?

This game is great for team building and problem solving as it requires everyone to participate and contribute towards the goal. Discussion and cooperation, reasoning, trial and error.

Smelly Trail

Preparation needed: collect together some smelly things. An adult need to go ahead and set the trails

Resources: fruit or vegetables with a distinct smell for instance onion, garlic, lemon, orange etc, a knife, a cloth for each fruit or vegetable being used

Age range: early years, primary, secondary, adult

Group size: either singularly or small groups

Additional issues: this is a great game for dividing groups

Send an adult or two ahead to lay the scent trails. Make sure you rub the smelly object for instance a strong-smelling onion on trees etc as you go. Keep rubbing every metre or so. Lead each smell to a different part of your 'home base'.

Rub the onion onto a square of cloth. Let the children smell it before they set off so they can match the smell.

If you lay another trail use a contrasting smell and do not let the two (or more scents) taint each other by keeping them well apart from each other.

If at the start you randomly divide your group by allowing alternate children to smell each cloth, you will hopefully have sorted groups at the end of the activity.

If you are working with older children or adults, you may want to try this blind folded as a group challenge.

At the end of the trail let the group find their smelly source, so an onion or an orange.

What are we learning from this activity?
Following a trail, using our olfactory senses, our sense of smell, health and safety outside, working solo or in a group, exploring the outdoor environment using senses other than sight.

Dragon Egg Hunt

Preparation needed: hide a cantaloupe melon in your school grounds, make a nest from sticks for it

Resources: cantaloupe melon

Age range: early years, primary

Group size: any

Additional issues: have a knife and plate handy to cut up the melon for a snack

Start your session with a story about the sighting of a dragon in your outdoor area the night before and tell the children that sometimes dragons land in quiet areas to lay an egg. Let the children explore the outdoor area and discover a hidden dragon egg tucked cosily in a stick nest. I like to decorate the melon with stick on jewels for an extra enchanted touch.

At the end of the session the children can enjoy a snack of 'Dragon Egg' melon.

What are we learning from this activity?
Storytelling, developing imagination, observational skills.

Barefoot Walk

Preparation needed: precheck area for sharp objects and litter

Resources: none

Age range: early years, primary, secondary, adult

Group size: any

Additional issues: you may want access to water or wet wipes after this activity especially if walking through mud. Do not do this activity in tick infested areas

Carefully check the area prior to the activity for sharp objects, litter and animal faeces. Remove shoes and socks. Slowly walk through different terrains for a sensory experience outside. Examples of terrains to experience are wet grass, pebbles, crunchy leaves, mud, sand, puddles and shallow streams. Talk to the participants about their expectation and then their experience. Did each area feel like you expected? What surprised you? Did you feel nervous or confident?

If your outdoor area does not have a range of terrains, why not set up your area to encompass them. Tough trays or tarpaulins work well. Why not ask the participants to close their eyes and lead them through the area?

What are we learning from this activity?
Talking and listening, theorising ideas, trying out and comparing actual experience to expectations.

Catapult Challenge

Preparation needed: collect items needed, find a range of pictures and diagrams, a working example is probably a good idea

Resources: mouse traps (I found a pack of 3 in a pound shop), duct tape, string, elastic bands, elastic, spoons, bicycle inner tubes, sticks, lolly sticks, marshmallows, seed bombs

Age range: primary, secondary, adult

Group size: small groups of 2-6 but as many groups as you need

Additional issues: mouse traps are quite dangerous so please supervise. Remove the trigger with pliers prior to starting. Make sure that 'missiles' are soft and fired away from people

Supply a range of resources as well as utilising natural resources around you. Making a catapult with a mousetrap is very easy. Remove the trigger wire first and tape a spoon onto the cross bar 'snap', pull back, put a soft missile (screwed up ball of paper, a marshmallow, a small seed bomb) onto the spoon and fire. A small mouse trap will project a marshmallow about 20-30 ft. Challenge the children to work in groups to build a better catapult that will fire an agreed missile. Ensure that trials are conducted by firing away from other groups. This is a good method to disperse wild flower seeds, (please see Seed Bomb activity description)

What are we learning from this activity?
Design and technology, problem solving, planning, trial and error, team work, working with others, building, constructing, potential energy, competing against others. Seed dispersal and looking after the environment by creating insect friendly habitats.

Worm Charming

Preparation needed: this activity works well on a damp day

Resources: collecting containers

Age range: early years, primary, secondary, adult

Group size: any

Additional issues: make sure that everyone is dressed for the weather

The idea of this activity is to literally charm the worms out of the ground. Divide the group into smaller groups and encourage them to collect as many worms from a defined area as possible.

Some children use singing as a method of encouraging worms to the surface, tapping, stamping, marching, dancing and hopping works well too. The children will need to work cooperatively and methodically to work out the best method of charming worms to them.

After an agreed length of time, maybe half an hour or so, tally up the number of worms gathered by each group. As a whole group, discuss the best methods for charming worms.

Maybe award prizes for completing the challenges. How about edible jelly worms? You can make these by bundling drinking straws into a mug, so they are packed together tightly, hold together with an elastic band and standing upright. Fill the straws with dissolved red jelly and pop in a fridge to set. When solid, warm the straws slightly by running under the hot tap and release the worms. Makes a great prize, however both morally and dietary they are not suitable for vegetarians.

What are we learning from this activity?
Cooperation with others, working out strategies, working at part of a team, problem solving.

Spider Obstacle Course

Preparation needed: gather resources

Resources: string, small bells or bottle tops, trees or fixed points, blindfolds

Age range: primary, secondary, adult

Group size: work in small groups of 6-8

Additional issues: make sure that the course is do-able for the size of the participants

Give each group a ball of string. They need to make a web maze making sure that there are holes and gaps big enough to get through but challenging enough to make it exciting. Incorporate opportunities to need to crawl, bend, stretch and jump within the web. Hang bells or bottle tops on strings. Take it in turns to make your way through the obstacle course. If you touch the strings the bells will ring. You can make it even more exciting by blindfolding one or two of the group and letting them touch the strings with their fingertips. If someone touches a string whilst completing they will feel the vibration on the string, the same as a spider and they can call out 'CAPTURED' and they need to go back to the beginning. Try swapping with another group and trying out their spiderweb.

What are we learning from this activity?
Working with others, problem solving, thinking about the needs and abilities of other people in the group, using senses of touch and hearing

Group Painting Challenge

Preparation needed: you will need to prepare the hoop in advance. A prepared sponge ball (see previous activity) is also needed

Resources: a hoop (of the hula hoop variety) string or para cord, a sponge ball, a bowl, paint, large paper/card or material, scissors

Age range: primary, secondary, adult

Group size: up to 12 works well but does work with bigger groups. If you have large groups, try having a couple of teams

Additional issues: none

Using four equal length strings, suspend a sponge ball from the centre of the hoop so it hangs about 30 centimetres below the hoop. Give everybody a piece of string about 2 metres long and ask them to tie it to the hoop, evenly spaced out.

Put paint or a mixture of mud and water into a bowl and lay out a large sheet of paper or material on the ground. You may want to draw an outline for them to paint or leave the team to decide on their own design.

Everybody needs to hold the end of their string. Nobody can touch the hoop. Make sure that all the strings are taut. As a team the group needs to coordinate their actions to dip the sponge ball into the paint and take it to the paper and paint on the paper by daubing the ball on the paper. This activity needs excellent communication between members of the group. If you have a large group have two teams and compare their paintings afterwards.

What are we learning from this activity?
Cooperation, working with others, communication, group art work.

Stone Stacking

Preparation needed: this activity works well in school grounds, woodlands and beaches

Resources: stones

Age range: primary, secondary, adult

Group size: any but ensure that there are sufficient resources. Some children may like to work in pairs

Additional issues: be aware that stone stacks are not always stable and so great care should be taken if using larger stones with little people

People have been building cairns which are piles of stones piled on top of each other since prehistoric times often marking significant spiritual places. Stone balancing has been practiced as a meditation exercise by some Buddhists and developed into an artform by some noteworthy artists including Andy Goldsworthy, Bill Dan and Adrian Gray. Look up Adrian Gray's website at www.stonebalancing.com for some inspirational photographs of his work.

When balancing stones start with making rock piles with the larger stones at the bottom and building the tower of stones finishing with the smallest stones at the top.

For rock balancing this is an effective way to focus concentration and soon becomes very addictive. The trick is to find the magical point where the stone balances. Try standing a stone on its end and see if you can find how to balance it. When you have achieved one, how about finding more, even balancing a stone on top of another balanced stone.

This is not an easy activity and some people have a better aptitude for it than others and in my experience, it does get a bit frustrating when you find that a nine year old child is far better than yourself at it, that being said, when you do manage to balance a stone not only is it aesthetically pleasing, the sense of achievement is enormous.

Make sure you take photographs, or no one will believe you!

What are we learning from this activity?
Patience, persistence, trial and error, balancing points, achieving personal goals, selecting natural resources.

The Importance of Reviewing your Sessions

As an outdoor learning practitioner, it is important to review and reflect on what happened in your session. Looking back over your time with the participants and thinking about what they took from each session, what went well, what failed and how the great bits could be improved or extended into further sessions will help you not only develop your own practice but also allow you to plan how you can make outdoor learning an even more positive and enjoyable experience for them next time. Look back and think about were all the participants suitably dressed for the session? This not only includes the children or young people but also the accompanying adults. If they were not comfortable throughout the session how could you improve their well being at subsequent sessions? Extra clothes, a shelter to cast shade or protect them from rain, is the area sheltered or does a chilly wind blow through it? Can you set up some screens (tarpaulin walls, willow screens or even strategic planting around the camp area)

Did the children get hungrier earlier than expected? Were there sufficient snacks and warm or cold drinks available?

Addressing any negative points as they arise will show the participants that you care and take on board their concerns.

Look at the activities and games you set up. Was there a good mixture or was it too craft heavy for the children who wanted to pursue more physical activities? Was there somewhere for a child who perhaps needed a little less hectic activity to go? Could you deploy your adults differently to cover the potential needs of all the members of the group?

At the end of a session (or even after each activity if appropriate) it is a great idea to ask the children how they enjoyed it and what they learned from it. I suggest looking at the work of Roger Greenaway who looks in more depth about reviewing with children. He suggests that reviewing activities with children and young people can remind them what they have achieved during the session and show that it was a valued experience. It can help them make sense and add meaning to their learning experience. By looking at an activity as a group they can get other perspectives which could help them to develop strategies to improve on what they did next time as well as reassuring them that it is ok to take risks and fail sometimes too.